Elective Home Education

Elective Home Education

Simon Webb

Trentham Books

Stoke on Trent, UK and Sterling, USA

Winner of the IPG DIVERSITY Award 2010

Trentham Books Limited
Westview House   22883 Quicksilver Drive
734 London Road   Sterling
Oakhill   VA 20166-2012
Stoke on Trent   USA
Staffordshire
England ST4 5NP

First published 2011

British Library Cataloguing-in-Publication Data
A catalogue record for this book is available from the British Library

ISBN: 978 1 85856 482 1

Designed and typeset by Trentham Books Ltd and printed in Great Britain by Henry Ling Ltd, Dorchester

Contents

Preface

I t is never easy to write with complete objectivity and detachment about an activity with which one is heavily involved. Because home education in the UK is at least as much a philosophical as an educational movement, it has been necessary to delve deeply into the beliefs of others and in the process perhaps reveal something my own opinions and prejudices.

This book is an account of the state of home education in the United Kingdom, with particular reference to the situation in England. This skewed perspective is motivated less by a blinkered and Anglocentric viewpoint than by the fact that Graham Badman's review of elective home education, which seems likely to have a profound effect on home education throughout the whole of the United Kingdom, took place in England. Any future legislation will also, at least initially, apply only in England. For this same reason, mention in the text to 'this country' will generally mean England, but on occasion the whole of the United Kingdom.

The English language renders it impractical to keep third person pronouns gender neutral. I can hardly refer to a child as 'it' and the current, barbarous custom of the illicit concordance of pronouns between singular and plural forms will not be adopted; there will be no referring to a single child as 'they' or 'them'. Instead, I have tried to alternate equally between 'she' and 'he', thus also avoiding the awkwardness and inelegance of writing 'he or she' each time.

I hope that readers will forgive my vanity in using occasional examples drawn from my own experience of home education, as these may be helpful in illustrating certain points. If anybody wishes to read more about home education or discuss the topics covered here in greater detail, I can be contacted on the blog: http://homeeducationheretic.blogspot.com/

1

Home education yesterday

One thing which everybody in the UK has in common is that they have all been to school. Well, almost everybody. Everybody except for a tiny handful of atypical individuals, our present Queen among them. In recent years the number of people who have been educated out of school has been growing. Slowly but inexorably, the numbers have increased until today there could be as many as eighty thousand children in Britain who do not go to school (Badman, 2009). The exact figure is impossible to determine, as we shall see. There is still some way to go before we reach the sort of levels seen in the USA, where around one and a half million children are home educated or 'home-schooled' (US Department of Education, 2008). If however the present upward trend continues, there is no telling how many home educated children there might be in ten or twenty years time.

School seems such a natural and integral part of modern life that it is easy to forget that the mass instruction of children in this way was rare for most of recorded history. Home education was the common practice until a few centuries ago. Throughout the period of the Old Testament, from perhaps two thousand BC until the time of Christ, the proper place for a child's education was the home (Gidney, 2003). The Bible contains many references to this. In the *Book of Proverbs* we find, ' Listen, my son, to your father's instruction and do not forsake your mother's teaching' (Proverbs, 1:8). The parents were recognised as the most important teachers for the child. This is no mere historical curiosity. Many home educating parents in the United States today are devout Christians who take such scriptural texts as divine backing for their decision to teach their own children.

Throughout the rest of the ancient world the practice was more for individual tuition or at the most the teaching of small groups, although schools did exist. An extremely early reference to formal education is to be found in a clay tablet dating from about 1700 BC which was unearthed in Iraq. It reads,

> The man in charge of Sumerian said, 'Why didn't you speak Sumerian?' He caned me. My teacher said, 'Your handwriting is unsatisfactory.' He caned me. I began to hate writing.

This is a view of conventional education which was to remain largely unchanged for almost four thousand years. Only a favoured few, the children of the wealthy, could expect to receive any sort of formal education in these settings. This remained the case, even in England, until the nineteenth century. The idea of educating children in institutions based in special buildings dates only from the middle ages. By the time of Elizabeth I, Shakespeare was writing in *As You Like It* of 'The whining schoolboy with his satchel and shining morning face, creeping like snail, unwillingly to school.' School as we understand it today had definitely arrived.

Only a small minority of children attended school in Shakespeare's day; perhaps one in eight (Cunningham, 2006). The proportion increased over the next few centuries until by Queen Victoria's reign many children of both sexes had at least a few years of schooling. The whole business was still fairly haphazard and completely voluntary. If a parent or child didn't fancy the idea, there was no more to be said. So in the middle of the nineteenth century, children as young as eight were still being sent up chimneys or down coal mines to earn a living. Often a child's wages could make the difference between survival and starvation for a poor family. They simply could not afford the luxury of a child sitting at a desk all day without earning a single penny.

Side by side with the slow move towards universal schooling which took place during the nineteenth century grew the tradition of home education; people chose to teach children at home despite the availability of schools. This was typified by the childhood of John Stuart Mill, the famous philosopher. His father was a proponent of what we would now call Hothousing, where a child's intellectual development is deliberately stimulated and accelerated with the intention, or at least hope, of producing a genius. James Mill accordingly taught his son at home from infancy. By three, the child was learning Greek. By eight, he had read Xenophon in the original and was learning Latin. He was carefully shielded from the influence of other children, meeting in general only adults. His academic achievements throughout adolescence were outstanding until, at the age of twenty, he suffered a nervous breakdown (Mill, 1873).

This sort of burnout is regarded by many modern home educators as more or less par for the course for childhoods like Mill's and has led parents today to be more cautious about pushing their children too hard. Although as we shall see, this reluctance to push a child academically can be taken to absurd lengths by some home educating parents.

Universal schooling in the UK began in 1870 with the passage of the Elementary Education Act, also known as Forster's Act from the name of the Liberal MP who was instrumental in its planning. This Act allowed local authorities to set up and run schools for children aged five to ten. These were called board schools. It was not until the passage of another Act in 1880 that attendance at school became more or less compulsory. From the beginning there was widespread opposition to the idea of universal, compulsory schooling for children.

The Newcastle Report into the State of Popular Education in England was published in 1861 and argued against compulsion in education. The authors of the report said:

> Any universal compulsory system appears to us neither attainable nor desirable. An attempt to replace an independent system of education by a compulsory system, managed by the government, would be met by objections, both religious and political... (Newcastle Report, 1861)

Many of the same objections to government sponsored compulsory education which were made at the time of the Newcastle Report are now being made by home educators who are vehemently opposed to the recommendations for regulating home education contained in the Review of Elective Home education in England, which was conducted by Graham Badman in 2009 (CSF select committee, 2009). These objec-

3

tions centre around the belief that the Government has no business to concern itself with what goes on in the family home. Parents are the guardians of their children; not the state.

There were other, more practical reasons for the widespread dissatisfaction which many felt for compulsory schooling. Since to begin with the new elementary schools were not free, parents were hit with a double financial penalty. Not only did they face the loss of a child's earnings, they were also forced to pay for the school! Little wonder that this caused huge resentment among working people. In the decade after the passing of the 1880 Education Act, prosecutions for the non-attendance of children at school were running at over a hundred thousand a year. It was the commonest offence in Britain, with the exception of drunkenness. It took the passage of a further Act in 1891, which made elementary board schools free, before the majority of parents accepted the situation and the custom of sending children to school became universal for the general population (Cunningham, 2006).

Meanwhile, the well-to-do carried on much as before. Home education remained an option for those who could afford to employ a governess or tutor. Parents who had the means to do so kept their children, boys and girls, at home until the age of ten. At that age, the boys would be sent to a boarding school, while the girls either attended school or continued to be home educated, usually by a governess. There were two reasons for the popularity of this form of home education. It was cheaper to keep a governess than send a girl to an expensive school and it was supposed that girls and boys needed quite different types of education. Good schools cost money and many parents saw little point in wasting all that money on girls. As one member of a Royal Commission on schools, the Schools Enquiry Commission observed in the mid nineteenth century: 'Boys are educated for the world, girls are educated for the drawing room' (Taunton Report, 1868). This custom and the thinking behind it continued well into the twentieth century.

For the first half of the twentieth century it was more or less taken as given that all children from families who could not provide a governess or tutor, would attend school. From time to time, cases cropped up in the courts which challenged this presumption. In a famous case in 1911, the courts upheld the right of parents not to send their children to school if they could provide an 'efficient' education at home. *Bevan v Shears* 1911, is important also for home educators in that it established that a local authority does not have the power to force a parent to send a child to school, except by going through the courts (Alverstone, 1911). This important case is examined in Chapter 5.

The age until which a child was required to remain at school gradually crept up from ten in 1870, to fifteen as established in the 1944 Education Act. It was the 1944 act which provided, quite inadvertently, the legal basis for the modern home education movement in Britain. Hidden away in the small print was a phrase which had probably been included as a nod to those who still preferred their children's education to be supervised by a governess or tutor. In Section 36 of the Act, it was laid down that parents must cause their children to receive a suitable education, 'either by regular attendance at school or otherwise' (Education Act, 1944). It is most unlikely that those who framed this legislation realised that these eight words would ultimately lead to many thousands of children being withdrawn from school to be taught by their parents. The legal basis for parents to teach their children at home was thus laid down by statute as early as 1944, although it had never actually been illegal to do so. It was almost a decade after the passage of the 1944 Act before anybody tried to claim this right in court.

In 1952, Joy Baker was living in Norfolk. She had had an unhappy time at school herself and decided that rather than entrust her children's education to school, she would prefer to undertake the job herself. So began a ten year battle with the local authority, which would mean that her four children were removed from her forcibly and made wards of court and she herself was fined several times and sentenced to two months imprisonment.

The truth is that educating children at home had always been the preserve of the wealthy and privileged. Nobody had ever imagined an 'ordinary' mother deciding to withdraw her children from school to teach them herself in this way. Perhaps with some vague memory at the back of their mind of the great struggle of the 1880s to enforce universal schooling upon all children and remembering the resistance this encountered, Norfolk County Council spent the next nine years doing everything in their power to force Mrs. Baker to send her children to school. Ultimately, they failed.

Between 1952 and 1961 when the courts finally decided in her favour, Joy Baker faced court case after court case, as her local authority repeatedly attempted to prove that her children could not possibly be receiving a 'suitable education' at home from their mother. There was widespread incomprehension that a housewife should feel that she could possibly be up to the task of teaching her own children. Her attempt to use the wording of the 1944 Education Act as justification for her actions was greeted with bewilderment: it was tacitly assumed by all concerned that the words 'either by regular attendance at school or otherwise' had been inserted into the 1944 Education Act not so that parents might teach their own children, but in order that those with money could engage governesses and tutors without the threat of the Truancy Officer turning up on the doorstep.

Time and again, magistrates tried to convince Mrs. Baker that she was wrong headed and was harming her children by keeping them out of school. The children were examined in court and attempts made to demonstrate their ignorance and lack of education. This led to an own goal by one magistrate. He asked Joy Baker's son, as a test of his general knowledge, what a camel had in its hump. The boy replied, 'fat.' Laughingly, the magistrate explained that he was quite mistaken and that anybody who had been properly educated would know that the hump contained water. To prove this, he sent for an encyclopaedia and discovered to his horror that the child had been correct and that he was wrong. (Baker, 1964).

Finally, in 1961 the courts ruled that the wording of the 1944 Education Act did give parents the right to educate their own children out of school. Joy Baker went on to write a book about her experiences called *Children in Chancery* (1964).

For the next fifteen years or so, a handful of families took advantage of the legal ruling and taught their own children at home. It was an uphill struggle because local education authorities simply could not understand why any parent would want to do such a thing. Most of the families were threatened with legal action and otherwise intimidated.

Other experiments in home education were taking place at this time. These included the so-called 'Free Schools' set up by groups of parents. Although this was essentially home education, several of these groups registered themselves with their local education authority as schools. Parents and volunteers took turns in supervising children in makeshift premises. These enterprises typically took place against a background of threats from local education welfare officers to prosecute parents for condoning their children's truancy (Head, 1974). A few years later in 1977, there were a few dozen home educating families in England and ten of them banded together to form the organisation Education Otherwise.

In the same year that Education Otherwise was founded, another court case had its beginnings a case which was to be just as significant in its own way as that of Joy Baker's, twenty years earlier. Mr Phillips and Ms Reah were the parents of a boy with the unusual name of Oak. They lived in Leeds and chose to educate their son at home. When the local education authority in Leeds at last became aware that Oak Reah was not attending school in the Summer of 1977, they wrote to his parents asking them about the educational provision being made for their son. His parents decided that it was nobody's business but their own and refused to give any information whatsoever about Oak's education. After a time the LEA grew impatient and issued a School Attendance Order.

A School Attendance Order means that parents have to send their child to a designated school. If they fail to do so, the local authority can prosecute them. They must then go to court and explain why their child is not at school and demonstrate that he is receiving a suitable education elsewhere. If the magistrates are not satisfied that a child is receiving an education the parents must register their child at a the named school. The law at that time said of the matter:

> If it appears to a local education authority that a child of compulsory school age in their area is not receiving suitable education, either by regular attendance at school or otherwise, they shall serve a notice in writing on the parent requiring him to satisfy them within the period specified in the notice that the child is receiving such education' (Education Act, 1944)

Having served a notice and received no answer, the local authority served a School Attendance Order on the family and then prosecuted Oak's parents. Oak Reah's parents mounted an ingenious defence to this. They argued that the local education authority was wrong to issue the School Attendance Order in the first place because it could not possibly have appeared to them that Oak was not receiving a suitable education: since they had no information at all about him, how could it appear to them that he wasn't receiving a suitable education?

Although the magistrate decided against them, Oak's parents sought a judicial review of his decision and in 1980 this was heard. Lord Donaldson decided that the LEA was quite justified in making enquiries of the parents and that although they were entitled to refuse to give any information about their son's education, the LEA might then very well decide to issue a School Attendance Order as a result. As we shall see, some parents still adopt this approach, giving their local authority as little information about their children's education as possible. It is rare today for such cases to end up in court.

The year before Education Otherwise was founded, another parent began home educating his daughter. Following in the tradition of John Stuart Mill's father, James, Harry Lawrence wished to turn his child into a genius. Fathers like this, for such people almost invariably are fathers, have seldom presented any problem for the authorities. It is always quite obvious that an education is taking place and the proud parent is rarely reluctant to talk about the project or describe his child's achievements. The provision of highly structured and carefully planned education of this sort, delivered in the form of one-to-one tutoring has never alarmed local authorities in the way that the softer and less rigorous teaching favoured by mothers does. Whether this preference is gendered is open to question.

The academic results of the home education which Ruth Lawrence received were astonishing. Like John Stuart Mill, she was kept from contact with other children by her father. At the age of eleven she began studying mathematics at Oxford University, completing her degree in two years rather than the usual three. Her final marks would have been enough to earn her two Firsts (Walmsley, 1987). Her father lived with her while she was at Oxford and when she was offered posts first at Harvard and later at Michigan University, he went with her to the United States. While there, she fell in love with a man almost thirty years her senior, about her father's age in fact. They married and moved to Israel. There are rumours that she actually resents her childhood education and feels that it was not a good idea.

The type of education which Harry Lawrence provided for his daughter – very intense, structured and academically demanding – is probably the exception among British home educators. Those who founded Education Otherwise followed a different educational philosophy. They were impressed with authors such as John Holt and Ivan Illich, both of whom argued that schools were damaging for children and that true education was best undertaken in the home. Whereas home educating parents such as James Mill and Harry Lawrence felt that school did not teach very effectively and that they could do better, the founders of Education Otherwise interpreted the word 'education' in an entirely different way. They saw it as in many ways the antithesis of schooling.

In the next chapter I explore what has variously been called 'unschooling', 'autonomous education', 'natural learning', 'child led learning' and 'informal learning'. Relevant here is the fact that the formal teaching of school subjects in a systematic way formed no part of what many of the home educating parents who started Education Otherwise thought of as real education. From its foundation Britain's main organisation for home educating parents had an ambivalent attitude towards conventional teaching. It had more in common with the sixties counter culture, rather than with stern Victorian ideas of cramming children full of facts.

One of the early inspirations for British home educators was Summerhill, the boarding school established in 1921 in the English county of Suffolk. This was a 'free' school, run upon democratic lines and with no compulsion at all (Neil, 1960). Even attending lessons was voluntary and those who wished to do so were free to play all day. This provided a model for the type of education envisaged by some of the founding members of Education Otherwise and the educational philosophy of Summerhill school is still a powerful force in home education as it is practiced in the United Kingdom.

There is no doubt that the ideas being developed and expounded by people like John Holt in the US at that time had a profound effect on those in the UK who were beginning to question the whole basis for the formal education of children in schools.

As early as 1962 Paul Goodman, an American university lecturer, published a book called *Compulsory Miseducation*, in which he argued that schools cause more harm than good and that true education is actually harmed by compulsory attendance at school. Two years later John Holt, a New York teacher, expounded a similar thesis in *How Children Fail*. He asserted that schools were damaging to children and that what went on in them had little to do with genuine education. He argued that children fail because education as it is delivered in schools is failing them. These books paved the way for serious thinking about the role and necessity of schools.

John Holt originally believed that the answer to children who failed at schools was the improvement of schools and a different approach to teaching. During the 1970s though, he became convinced that this did not go far enough. The problem lay not in the type of school, or the methods of teaching used there. The problem was school itself (Holt, 1981). At the same time that Holt was coming to this radical conclusion, a husband and wife team of researchers, Raymond and Dorothy Moore, were heading towards the same idea from a slightly different direction.

The Moores were carrying out academic research on the Early Childhood Education movement. To begin with, their findings called into question the effectiveness of the conventional teaching of young children as carried out in nurseries and schools. This soon led to the surprising notion that not only was such teaching ineffective; it was positively harmful to the child's development. They wrote, and in 1975 published, a book called *Better Late then Early*, in which they suggested that formal education was best delayed until the age of twelve or so. Later, they became advocates of home education.

By 1981, the idea of home education was firmly established in the USA. That year John Holt published *Teach Your Own* and the Moores published *Home Grown Kids*. These books gave encouragement to parents in the UK who were hoping to educate their own children at home. They also provided a theoretical foundation for the practice of a different kind of home education. This new model of home education had little in common with the Gradgrindian approach of fathers such as James Mill or Harry Lawrence. It was instead predicated on the assumption that children could learn simply by being with their parents and joining in everyday life and activities. The work of the Moores, for instance, was backed by solid research which demonstrated the advantages to young children of being with a loving caregiver, rather than in an impersonal classroom.

Iris Harrison, one of the founder members of Education Otherwise and a believer in some of the ideas outlined above, faced legal action from her local authority in 1977. Her case has many of the features that typify modern home education and so it is worth examining. Her children had difficulties with reading and writing. Today, we would probably describe them as dyslexic, but thirty years ago they were provisionally diagnosed as being 'educationally sub-normal'. This prompted Mrs Harrison and her husband Geoff to make the almost unheard of decision to withdraw their children from school in order to teach them at home. Her local education authority took the family to court, insisting that the Harrisons were condoning their children's 'truancy'.

Part of the local authority's concern was that the Harrisons had a much broader definition than the average school of what constituted an education. They were both happy for their children to spend their days playing the violin or tinkering with machinery, rather than studying traditional subjects like history, geography and English literature. (Harrison, 1981) It was the unconventional nature of the family's lifestyle, coupled with what was seen as a risk of social isolation, which caused the local authority to take the family to court. The children may well have been learning but the local authority were not convinced that they were being *taught*.

Eventually in 1981, the case reached Worcester Crown Court. The judgement reached grudgingly allowed the Harrisons to continue educating their children themselves. The judge in the case defined a 'suitable education', the words from the 1944 Education Act, as one which would, 'Prepare children for life in modern civilised society and enable them to achieve their full potential'. This definition has not changed over the last thirty years or so, although it may soon be superseded by a more rigorous definition, as this is currently under discussion in the Department for Education.

There are two significant points about the case of the Harrison children and both are still relevant to home education in Britain today. The decision to home educate the children was taken not because Mr and Mrs Harrison were enthusiastic about the idea of teaching their own children. After all, they were happy to send them to school to begin with. They were responding to problems with the school and how the children were treated there. This is a recurring theme today. It is still relatively rare to hear of children whose parents educate them from the age of five right through until sixteen. Inadequate provision for special educational needs and disabilities, problems with bullying, school phobia and school refusal; all these are common reasons for parents to de-register their children from school (Rothermel, 2002; Hopwood *et al*, 2007).

The second important aspect of Iris Harrison's story is the type of education which she proposed to give her children. There was no question here of a child learning Greek at three or entering Oxford University at eleven. It was decided by the parents that the actual style of education being offered by the school was not suitable for their children. They wanted them to be able to develop according to their own interests, as opposed to conforming to an externally imposed curriculum. One of the children was keen on the violin; she should be free to play her violin as much as she wished, not have to stop at a predetermined time to study physics or chemistry. One of their sons preferred working with his hands to academic study. He too must be able to follow his own inclinations. Essentially, this is what has become known in recent years as 'autonomous home education'. It is enormously popular among British parents who home educate. This strange and apparently counterintuitive notion is discussed in the next chapter.

Following the two key decisions in *Phillips v Brown* in 1980 and *Harrison and Harrison v Stevenson* in 1981, the stage was set for the rapid growth of home education in the UK. It had been established that the practice was lawful and that the 1944 Education Act could in fact be used in support of home education. In a sense, the floodgates were now open.

This did not stop a number of local education authorities from fighting a fierce rearguard action against allowing home educators to withdraw their children from school. Few people had heard of the rulings in these cases so it was easy for local authorities to mislead parents into believing either that home education was illegal or that the authority had great powers to regulate or restrict the form it took. Neither proposition is true, although this does not prevent some local authorities even today from making similar claims. Throughout the 1980s the number of home educators grew slowly but steadily. It was not until the mid 1990s that the pace quickened, until by the new millennium numbers were growing exponentially (BBC, 2005). Again, this mirrored but lagged a little behind the situation in America. In the United States there were estimated to be no more than a few thousand children being educated at home in the 1960s. Today, the figure is between one and a half and two million. Most of this huge growth took place during the 1990s. At least part of this phenomenal growth over the last ten or fifteen years is due to the influence of the Internet.

The Internet is crucial to home educating parents. At one time information about important developments such as the judgement at Worcester Crown Court would need to have been tracked down in libraries or obtained by joining an organisation such as Education Otherwise. By the end of the 1990s, all this was available at the click of a mouse.

Being a home educating parent can be a lonely and isolating endeavour, particularly for those who live outside the big cities. The Internet provided, in addition to practically unlimited information on the subject of home education, access to online communities of like minded souls. On such sites, parents found that they could ask questions, express anxieties, seek advice and encourage one another. Hints and tips could be exchanged about various local education authorities and the best way of dealing with them. More, they could instantly contact home educators in other countries, exchanging notes with them about threats to their lifestyle. The Internet has revolutionised home education.

All of which brings us to the present day. As we have seen, home education is not a new idea: it is found in writings some 3000 years old. We have sketched the development of the idea and shown how the foundations for the modern day home education movement in Britain were laid and the legal basis established through a few key cases of precedent. It is time to look at how home education is actually carried out in the UK today.

To do this, we need to look not so much at facts, figures and statistics, but rather at the fallible ideas and fancies of real people. This means that any account is liable to be biased and idiosyncratic. I hope to present the points of view of the various parties fairly, but what follows is written from the perspective of somebody who spent many years home educating in a largely structured and academic way and this will probably colour my account. It also important to remember that home education is currently in a state of flux. A recent attempt to introduce new legislation to control home education failed due to the calling of an election in May 2010: however, it seems likely that the law will change in some way over the next few years. It is impossible to say what form any such change might to take.

2

The situation today

A ny account of home educating in England today must begin with Graham Badman's review of elective home education. We look closely at this in Chapter 5, but for now it is enough to give a brief description of the review and its aftermath. In January 2009 the Secretary of State for Education asked Graham Badman, former Director of Children's Services in Kent, to review the arrangements for home education in England. Badman saw many witnesses and received a huge number of written submissions. He published his report in June 2009 and recommended that home education should be regulated more tightly and that certain restrictions should be placed upon the practice (Badman, 2009).

Publication of the report and its recommendations was welcomed by the Department for Children, Schools and Families (DCSF), who announced that they accepted Badman's findings and intended to implement all his recommendations fully. Some home educating parents and support groups reacted angrily and the CSF select committee undertook a brief review of the conduct and findings of Badman's review. This took place in October 2009 and with a few minor exceptions, they endorsed his conclusions (CSF select committee, 2009).

Nobody knows how many children in the UK are educated at home. According to a study commissioned by the government in 2006, nobody can know! (Hopwood *et al*, 2007). The reason for this is simple; those educating their own children have never been obliged to tell anybody of their plans. All that has been necessary is for parents not to send their child to school at the age of five. There has never been a requirement to register with the local authority or discuss the matter with anybody. The situation is different when a child is at school and then de-registered by the parents. In such a case, the school will usually notify the local authority, who will become aware that one more child in their area is being taught at home. This makes it impossible to do more than guess the total number of home educated children.

There have been several attempts in recent years to try to find out how many home educated children there are in Britain. Between August and November 2006, York Consulting Ltd. undertook a study for the Department of Education and Science, which in May 2010 became the Department for Education. Their brief was to examine elective home education in England and try to identify any perceptible trends. In particular, to use the words of the subsequent report, 'The aim of the study was to assess the viability of determining the prevalence of home education in England' (Hopwood et al, 2007).

They were asked to find out whether it was possible to count the number of home educated children in Britain. The main conclusion of the study, which was published the following spring was is that 'it is not feasible to reliably ascertain the prevalence of home educated children through a national survey of LAs and home education organisations' (Hopwood et al, 2007).

The reason no one knows how many children are being taught at home is that many parents see no need to notify their local authority when they begin to teach their own children. The York Consulting study and Badman's review of elective home education conducted in 2009 came to broadly similar conclusions: local authorities in England know of between fifteen to twenty thousand children who are educated at home but acknowledged that there are many more who are unknown to the local authorities. The question is: how many more?

Estimates of the total number of children who are home educated vary wildly. One piece of research suggested that the total number of home educated children was a little more than double that known to the local authorities (Fortune-Wood, 2005). This would give a figure of perhaps forty thousand, a number favoured by the local authorities themselves. But home educating support groups say it could be more like fifty or sixty thousand, while in his report on elective home education carried out for the DCSF, Badman talks of as many as eighty thousand (2009). Even more extravagant claims have been made, that the true figure is closer to one hundred and fifty thousand (*Guardian*, 2000). The truth is that nobody knows. All that most researchers feel able to say with assurance is that there are at least twenty thousand and probably many, many more.

However, even this generally agreed figure may be unreliable. In November 2009 a group of local authority officers met with members of the Children, Schools and Families select committee. When the question of the total number of home educated children known to local authorities was raised, it was mentioned that the numbers fluctuate throughout the year (CSF select committee, 2009). According to Ofsted's report, *Local authorities and home education* (2010) variation in numbers throughout the year can be dramatic. One authority's figure was 630 home educated children in September, at the beginning of the school year, but that this dropped by about a third to 430 or so by the spring.

The reason for these fluctuations is simple. Parents might begin home educating their children after the summer holidays but find by Christmas that the job is more than they bargained for, so their children start school the following January. Since there is no fixed point in the school year at which censuses are conducted of home educated children known to the local authority, the widely quoted figure of twenty thousand may be misleading. Of, say, twenty thousand home educated children counted in September, there could be as few as fourteen thousand by the beginning of the following year.

Badman observed that if he were working for a local authority which knew so little about the children being educated within its boundaries, he would be dissatisfied with the information (Badman, 2009). Imagine for a moment such a local authority. How many children of school age does it contain? Perhaps twenty, but perhaps eighty thousand. Well, maybe more – nobody has counted. How many of these children have special educational needs? Can you tell us how many of these children achieved five GCSEs between the grades of A* and C in the last year? And what about ethnic breakdown or the number entitled to free school meals?

In fact little is known about home educated children and their families in England. Different people make different guesses, depending upon their agenda. The guesses however remain just guesses with few hard facts upon which to work. Even for those registered with local authorities, reliable information is sparse. Name, age, perhaps ethnic origin and some idea of the parents' methods: that's about all. Even basic information, such as how many GCSEs are taken and passed, is lacking. Local authority involvement with a home educated child ends officially on the last Friday in June of the academic year in which the child becomes sixteen. GCSE results are received that August and there is no reason why home educating parents should then notify their local authorities of these results. Many don't do so.

Why do parents choose to educate their children at home rather than send them to school? The answer is frequently bound up with the hostility many home educating parents feel towards both schools in general and their local authority in particular. They cannot fail to see how tensions can arise between them and the local authority because they have chosen to home educate their children.

The first broad distinction to make is between parents who choose to undertake the education of their children as a positive decision and those who feel compelled to do so. In his report on home education, Graham Badman distinguished between true elective home education and what he called, 'home education by default' (Badman, 2009). Taking the first group:

- Parents such as Harry Lawrence make a conscious decision to educate their own children because they feel they can make a better job of it than any school. They do not send their children to school in the first place so seldom become known to their local authority.

- In contrast to parents who worry that schools are insufficiently rigorous and academic, there are those who feel that schools are too rigorous and intense, and wish their children to have a gentler and more relaxed childhood, learning at their own pace. They are anxious about the constant testing of children throughout their school life and feel that this puts children under too much pressure. Many autonomously educating parents feel like this.

■ Still others are uneasy about the influence other children might have upon their offspring. This can be for cultural or religious reasons; a number of Christians, Muslims and Jews educate their children at home in to keep them from what they see as the negative influence of children from irreligious backgrounds. A sizeable number of Gypsy/Roma families prefer their children not to attend school for some of the same reasons (Ivatts, 2006).

■ Yet others are proponents of 'attachment parenting', where parents keep their child closer to them than is considered normal in today's society. All these parents have made a positive choice, for various reasons, that they will assume responsibility for the education of their own children and will not send them to school. According to Rothermel (2002), only 30 per cent of such parents in this category always intended to educate their own children.

■ Then there are the parents who, like Iris Harrison, withdraw their children from school after initially sending them, because they think the school is not providing enough help for difficulties their child is facing. Typical reasons for withdrawal are bullying and the perceived inadequacy of provision made for a child's special educational needs (Hopwood *et al*, 2007).

■ Bullying might account for as much as a third of home education in England and Wales (Ofsted, 2010). In some cases the two major reasons overlap: a child is bullied because of a disability or special need, or is on the autistic spectrum and looks normal but behaves oddly. Often, as in the case of the Harrisons, the special educational need is relatively minor, such as dyslexia or hyperactivity.

■ There are also the children who become so stressed or depressed by the experience of school that they refuse to attend. This is described as 'School Phobia' or, more neutrally, 'School Refusal'. These children are frequently de-registered soon after starting either primary or secondary school. In a sense, these parents are not choosing to home educate. They say they had no choice, that there was nothing else they could do but take this step. These are the sort of cases which Badman meant when he talked of 'home education by default'.

- Another category are those parents who have de-registered their children from school to avoid prosecution for truancy or the child's permanent exclusion. Nobody knows how prevalent this might be.

- Finally, there are parents who approve in principle of schools but are dissatisfied with their local school. If they cannot get their children into a school they are happy with, they sometimes de-register their children, whether as a protest to try and force the hand of a local authority or because they so dislike the particular school that they feel reluctantly compelled to teach their children themselves.

In many cases the decision to withdraw the child from the school is made following an acrimonious dispute or, more frequently, a series of acrimonious disputes. Parents are fiercely protective of their children's interests and when they form the impression that a school is not keeping their child safe from harm they are likely to become angry and distressed. Parents whose children are being bullied at school frequently blame the school for not tackling the problem or failing to treat it with what they see as appropriate urgency. The decision to de-register a child from school under these circumstances is therefore often accompanied by a good deal of anger at the school's perceived shortcomings and most likely also the local authority.

Parents whose children refuse school become similarly angry when they meet with an insufficiently sympathetic response from the school to persistent lateness or unauthorised absences (Chitty, 2008). Here too, the decision to withdraw the child from school is generally the culmination of a series of fraught meetings with staff from the school and perhaps Education Welfare Officers and psychologists. Just as in the case of the bullied child, the stage is set for confrontation in any subsequent dealings with what parents see as 'The Authorities'.

Many professionals in the field of education do not accept that so-called 'School Phobia' is a genuine syndrome (Furedi, 2009). They feel that dignifying a child's reluctance to go to school as a medical condition is absurd. We saw in Chapter 1 the Elizabethan schoolboy 'creeping like snail, unwillingly to school'. Could this be the first recorded instance of school phobia? Or could it just be the feeling we all have at times towards things that we are compelled to do? Is there such a syndrome as work phobia perhaps? The expression 'school refusal' is a preferable term.

Parents may also resent the school and the local authority's reluctance to deal with the child's special educational need. This is likely to apply to what are regarded as fairly minor difficulties such as dyslexia, ADHD or dyspraxia, not a severe disability. If the parents of such children see the school as unsympathetic and as failing to give their children the special consideration they deserve, they may withdraw their child as part of the endgame in a bitter dispute with the school and educational support services.

These reasons for choosing to home educate do not make for a harmonious or cordial relationship between parents and local authorities. Leaving aside the rights and wrongs of the matter, parents feel they and their children have been let down and betrayed by the schools, local authorities and 'the system' in general. They frequently say that they want no more to do with the educational establishment because the schools and local authority refused to help them when they asked them to, so they refuse to co-operate with them in future. If the authorities wish to know what they are doing now, they won't tell them.

The problem is that the engagement of the parents with the local authority does not and cannot end at the point where the child is de-registered from school. Once the child is no longer at school, the local authority needs to be assured that she is receiving a fulltime education 'suitable to her age and aptitude' elsewhere. And this is where the trouble can begin.

Ultimately, a local authority which believes that a child within its area is not being educated can issue a School Attendance Order, after it has enquired of the parents as to the nature of the educational provision being made for their child. If the response is unsatisfactory, the local authority can, after issuing the School Attendance Order, prosecute the parents. Local authorities tend to be sparing in their use of School Attendance Orders (CSF select committee, 2009; Ofsted 2010).

As we saw in Chapter 1, before they can issue one it must appear to them that a child is not receiving a suitable education. Home education in itself is not sufficient grounds to lead to this supposition, as parents are swift to point out. However, in the case we looked at earlier, *Phillips v Brown* 1980, in which parents refused to respond to enquiries from their local authority about the educational provision being made for their son, the judge gave his opinion that local authorities were entitled to make what he called 'informal enquiries'. If these proved fruitless and parents would provide no information at all, the local authority might be entitled to draw an unfavourable conclusion about the quality of education being provided for the child.

Shortly after a child has been withdrawn from school, a letter from the local authority is likely to land on the doormat. The exact wording of this letter varies from place to place. Typically, it will request the opportunity to visit the home and speak to parents and child about the future plans for the child's education. Sometimes a form is included for parents to fill out. Of course, at least for the moment, local authority officers have no automatic right of access to either the home or the child. From the perspective of an Education Welfare Officer, the request for such a meeting may seem quite natural and straightforward, but to a mother who has watched her child suffering for months without being offered any practical help and assistance, it can be the last straw. And so the seeds of conflict may be sown.

The parents do not stand to gain in material terms from taking their child out of school. The thousands of pounds which the local authority receives from central government for every pupil registered at school, the Age Weighted Pupil Unit, ceases when the child is de-registered. There is no money to help parents with educating their child. Parents who teach their own children become solely responsible for the entire enterprise. Everything from visits to the swimming pool to the cost of arranging GCSEs for their children must be paid for by the parent. When we realise that sitting a single GCSE as a private candidate at a school or college can cost around £150, we can see that home education is liable to impose a considerable financial burden on a family. Even if money were available, parents might find it difficult to gain access to the exam. By the time the final step of de-registration has been reached, schools are often exasperated by what they might see as a demanding and perhaps unreasonable parent and are glad to see the back of them and their child.

When, for example, the parents of children with special educational needs de-register children who are receiving Speech and Language Therapy and various other services, they can find that such help ends as soon as they withdraw their child because these services are usually delivered through the school. Enquiries to the school may be met dismissively. When the school encounters the hostility parents who have de-registered their children from school generally feel, the chances of an amicable arrangement being made with such home educating parents by their local authority are slender. Ofsted noted examples of this situation in the survey of home education it published in 2010. A mother whose child was receiving physiotherapy while registered at school mentioned that she was considering home education. She was told that it was a case of 'either school and services or home education and nothing' (Ofsted, 2010). Other parents confirmed that this attitude was common.

For those who do not wish to receive a visit from a local authority officer, the most popular gambit is to supply them with an 'Educational Philosophy'. Such a document is particularly favoured by autonomously educating parents. The difficulty with such evidence from the point of view of the local authority is that it does not actually tell them what the child is learning or even doing. It is easy enough to download an Ed Phil, as they are know for short, from an Internet site and then to personalise it. The end result might say something along the lines of:

> Our approach to John's education is in the main opportunity-based, child-led and very flexible. It is impossible to provide a timetable or to specify in advance which activities we shall be undertaking. We work to keep a good balance between child-led, informal learning and a more directed approach. In general, it is our aim to facilitate learning through John's interests rather than artificially contrived situations to reach pre-determined outcomes. We are always vigilant for any gaps which should arise in our provision and ready, willing and able to make the necessary adjustments to fill them.

This might continue for several pages. The first thing to strike the impartial reader is that it carefully avoids saying anything definite. What is John actually doing? Is he learning to read at a level appropriate to his age and commensurate with his abilities? We are not told. Will he sit examinations? Impossible to say. What about maths or history? Science?

Nobody knows. It is not hard to see why many local authorities are profoundly dissatisfied with such a document. What can they do about it? Should they issue a School Attendance Order and then take the parents to court?

There is certainly nothing in the above statement to suggest that a suitable education is not being provided – and it may well be. But without visiting the home and talking to the child and his parents, it is impossible to be sure. The child might be an infant prodigy or he may be completely non-verbal, wheelchair bound and suffering from severe learning difficulties. Then again, she may be a child of normal ability who is not really being taught at all. Or he could be an ordinary child studying for five GCSEs. How can we possibly tell from reading the 'educational philosophy'?

This is the bind into which local authority officers charged with the monitoring of home education find themselves caught time and again. This desire to visit the home and speak to the child is currently one of the main causes of friction between some home educators and their local authorities. It also touches upon another important issue in the home education debate: the extent to which the monitoring of home educators is a question of safeguarding, rather than monitoring education *per se*. Parents point out, with some justification, that the hour or two of access to their homes once a year which is typically requested by local authorities is wholly insufficient to establish the quality of the education being received by the child. They are probably right.

The most a short visit might achieve is to reassure the local authority that the parent is not mentally ill, the child is not being kept from school in order to work, and that the home circumstances are not so dreadful as to require intervention from social services. With luck, there might be a chance to hear the child read out loud and perhaps see some written work. It is often possible when glancing around a home to form some impression as to whether a child is receiving an education. Are there plenty of books? Are there magazines and newspapers lying around? These can be reassuring indicators that the child is being raised in a home where learning and education are nurtured. Or are the children slumped in front of the television in their pyjamas at lunchtime? Is the only reading material in sight a shop catalogue? None of this is conclusive evidence, and some home educating parents dismiss such casual judgement of their lifestyle as simply snobbishness.

There is another anxiety on the part of local authorities, one which is seldom articulated and has nothing to do with either the welfare of the child or the quality of education she is receiving. It is more a question of local authorities covering their backs. Every day we read of somebody suing somebody else for bizarre reasons. Local authorities are routinely sued because somebody has tripped on an uneven or badly maintained paving stone. More recently, we have seen children attempting to take legal action against schools because they were bullied at school or because their individual needs were not met (BBC, 2002). One of the great fears of local authorities is that a formerly home educated person will become aggrieved as an adult because the education he received from his parents was inadequate and will attempt to sue the local authority because they failed to scrutinise and monitor his education closely enough.

No such case has been brought, but it is a possibility. Since the duties and responsibilities of local authorities which touch upon home education are so loose and open to varying interpretation, it is felt that a proper definition of suitable, full-time and efficient education would cut the ground away from the feet of anyone trying to bring an action on these grounds.

Some children have been removed from school supposedly to be educated at home but in fact to avoid either permanent exclusion or the prosecution of parents for their child's truancy. Unfortunately, schools and local authorities sometimes collaborate with parents in this sham to rid themselves of undesirable pupils. This is known as off-rolling, and the aim for the school may be to avoid looking bad by having high exclusion or truancy statistics. For parents, the motive is clear: they do not want to be prosecuted or have their child stigmatised by permanent exclusion. This practice is the subject of Recommendation 15 of Badman's report. He urged that:

> The DCSF take such action as necessary to prevent schools or local authorities advising parents to consider home education to prevent permanent exclusion or using such a mechanism to deal with educational or behavioural issues. (Badman, 2009)

In 2000 a school in Newcastle was revealed to have hit upon a scheme for getting rid of its difficult pupils and persistent truants. Parents were instructed to sign letters de-registering their children and claiming that they intended to educate them at home. There was never any intention to do so: the whole thing had been dreamed up by the school in order to off-roll some of its less desirable pupils (Davies, 2000). No doubt this still happens, but it is impossible to say how prevalent it is (CSF select committee report, 2009). Sometimes little effort is made to monitor the education such children are receiving at home. Typically, they are fourteen and fifteen year-old boys who, when they are not truanting, are disruptive and troublesome at school. The schools are not eager to have them back and the local authority would like to avoid having a to spend a fortune in catering for them elsewhere. The fact that Badman made a specific recommendation about this practice suggests that the off-rolling of pupils in this way, to be supposedly educated at home, is common practice.

A group of local authority officers who gave evidence to the Department of Children Schools and Families select committee in October 2009 suggested that one peak in deregistration from school was between the ages of thirteen and fifteen, during the run up to GCSEs (CSF select committee, 2009). It is likely that several factors are at work here. On the one hand, many parents are genuinely concerned about the stress that studying for ten or twelve GCSEs might cause their children. There is also the natural friction between parents and teenagers about homework and school. It must sometimes appear to parents that if school were removed from the equation, life would be a lot easier and there would be less conflict between them and their children. No more insisting on early bedtimes, no more shouting at the child to get her up in the mornings, no more fights over homework: the advantages are clear, at least in the short term. It is hard to state with certainty what motivates parents to de-register their children from school at this age but it seems likely that self-interest and the avoidance of trouble with their children play at least some part in the decision.

So much for those children whose parents felt that they had little choice but to choose home education. What of parents who decide as a positive choice that they will assume responsibility for their children's education? These may well constitute the majority of home educators. If there are really at least as many children being home educated as are actually known to the local authorities, most of them are probably children who never even started school. This would explain why they are unknown to their local authority: they have never been on a school roll. Others have just moved from one district to another so have fallen from sight in that way. What of such children?

Some of these children are doubtless being taught methodically and intensively by parents who are dedicated to their children's education. They teach their children to read and write, they cover mathematics systematically and also explore history, geography and science. There are still many fathers and mothers with views like those of the parents of John Stuart Mill and Ruth Lawrence. The reason that such home educators have never notified the local authority of their existence is because they just want to get on with the job and are aware that there is unlikely to be any practical assistance from the local authority. Some are individualists who resent any interference in their lives and methods. They know they can do a better job than modern schools and they see no point in involving themselves in monitoring or visits. Many more of those who are unknown are autonomous educators who do not register themselves with the local authority because they prefer to remain 'under the radar', as they call it. They do not want anything to do with the educational system and are in many cases vehemently opposed to what they call 'coercive learning' – more often known as conventional teaching.

Autonomous education

Autonomous education is one of the main strands of British home education and the method of education most likely to bring parents into conflict with their local authority. In the wake of Badman's report on elective home education in England, autonomous home educators have been leading the opposition to any change in the current legal position for parents who educate their own children.

The expression 'autonomous education' was coined by Jan Fortune-Wood who, together with her husband, educated their own four children at home. They founded what has become one of the largest home education support groups in the country, Home Education UK. Autonomous education is similar to, but not precisely the same, as what

Americans call unschooling and others child-led, natural or informal learning. Essentially, it means that the child alone is in control of her own learning and choosing what she will learn, when and how. The parents may make suggestions, and facilitate experiences, even teach if requested to do so, but the driving force behind the whole process is the child and her wishes.

For schoolteachers, this is a strange concept that is liable to make them feel ill at ease, as it runs counter to much of the received wisdom on the subject of education. An education without a curriculum or plan, a child not being directed and supervised in his learning, even the acquisition of literacy being left to the whim of a five-year old. It sounds preposterous to me. But the only question to ask of any pedagogic technique is not whether it offends our sensibilities and differs from much of what we believe about teaching but: does it work? The answer in this case is, 'Yes ... sometimes.'

A problem lies at the heart of this whole notion of autonomous learning. It causes some to think that when an autonomously educated child does pick up the sort of vital knowledge which she will surely need if she is to take her rightful place as an adult in a modern, industrial society, she is doing so in spite of, rather than because of the way she is being raised and educated.

At the heart of the theory of autonomous education lies what many see as a faulty piece of logic. It is based on a faulty analogy, which is this: because children will do some things naturally and acquire some skills without formal instruction, they are liable to do other, different things naturally and acquire a raft of other skills without being taught them. So just as the growing and developing child will 'learn' to walk and talk, so too will she 'learn' to read, write and perform arithmetical operations. This is a plausible, easily understood and attractive idea and, as so often the case with plausible, easily understood and attractive ideas, it may be quite wrong (Hirsch, 2006).

Human babies are born pre-programmed with various potentials and inherent abilities. One of these is the ability to move around like other members of their species. They do not have to be taught to do this: like most animals, they will do it as a matter of course, just as a newborn foal will stand and walk around shortly after birth, without being taught by another horse. This is a natural development of being born a horse.

The ability to speak is similarly hard wired into the baby's brain. He will need to learn the words of the language used around him, but will not need to be taught to speak. If the young child can acquire the ability to stand up and then walk and talk so naturally, surely she can acquire literacy in the same natural way? Perhaps mathematics can be also learned like this? History and geography? Perhaps even science? It is an enticing idea and could mean that schools are wholly unnecessary. However, the two processes are entirely different.

There is nothing 'natural' about alphabetic scripts. Everything about them is artificial and bears no relation to anything in the natural world. Breaking words down into little pieces, scanning rapidly from left to right, silent letters: all this is a human invention and a relatively recent one (Hirsch, 2006). The same goes for mathematics, only far more so. Base ten arithmetic, place value, binary code: these are all inventions of the human mind, completely divorced from the natural world.

Consider one small aspect of mathematics, that of place value. Here is number 136 and here is number 387. Now the interesting bit is that the number 3 in the second string of digits is actually worth ten times the value of the number 3 in the first number. This notion has only been around for a few centuries. A child may, a year or so after birth, stand up without anybody teaching him to do so. He will not, even if he lives to be a hundred, devise place value. That is because it is transmitted not in DNA but by culture. It must be learned. No learning, no place value. To be more precise, it must be learned by being taught. The chances of a child staring at strings of digits and working out for herself the mechanism of place value are not high.

For this reason most people would agree that education is vital to children from early on. It is a completely artificial process, which entails older members of the species passing on knowledge which they feel that the younger one should know. The more systematically and efficiently this is done, the better for the child. We often try and disguise that this is happening by using metaphors that suggest a natural event. We talk about the child's mind as developing or growing. Trees grow and fruit develops, but If a child's mind changes it is usually because we have caused the change to happen. We have educated her!

Autonomous educators believe that the most important aspect of a child's learning is that the child should be learning for the sake of it, for the intrinsic pleasure in finding things out and discovering the world around him. They contrast this with the essentially extrinsic motivation to be found in classrooms, where the child is rewarded for certain behaviours and incurs sanctions for others. They assert that it is intrinsic learning which will stay with a child, rather than the sterile contents of an externally imposed curriculum.

It has been necessary to look closely at the idea of autonomous education to see why parents who raise their children in this way deny the need for a curriculum and are opposed to providing even the sketchiest outline of their plans for the coming year. They cannot speculate upon the direction and extent of their child's learning in the next twelve months lest this limit and stunt the child's 'natural' development.

We have seen that one of the causes of the phenomenal growth in home educating is parental dissatisfaction with schools and local authorities and that a major cause of local authority dissatisfaction with home educating parents is their persistent refusal to provide plans, curricula, marked work and detailed records of their children's education and learning. Many local authority officers suspect that many of the children who are not at school are not receiving any sort of education. In submissions to Badman's review and also in evidence to the CSF select committee, some local authorities estimated that a substantial proportion of children being educated at home are receiving an inadequate education or none at all (Badman Report 2009; CSF select committee, 2009).

Natural and gentle learning, this romanticised view of childhood learning, has only been around in its current form since the Enlightenment. It is an attractive philosophy, so much more agreeable than the idea of forcing hard facts into a babyish brain. It's much more natural. Autonomous home education has its roots in the philosophy of men like Karl Popper. Popper wrote of his own school days, '...we were wasting our time shockingly, even though our teachers were well-educated and tried hard to make the schools the best in the world' (Popper, 1976). He later expounded the view that true education is quite the opposite of formal schooling, an opinion eagerly taken up by autonomously educating parents.

This sort of education also draws inspiration from experiments such as Summerhill school. The basic idea is that if children learn things that they want to learn, they will find this enjoyable and learn far more effectively than if they are coerced by an adult. This desire to learn which comes from the child himself is described as 'intrinsic' motivation. When a child learns because she is made to, autonomous educators call this 'coercive learning' and regard it as being by definition a bad thing. So what if the child does not want to learn to read? What if she just wants to watch television all day? What about children who have little intrinsic motivation and do not wish to learn anything? All these are fair points and ones which local authority officers who monitor home education regularly raise.

Some academics argue that it is possible for small children to learn to read and acquire mathematical ability with no formal instruction. Dr. Alan Thomas, Visiting Fellow at the University of London Institute of Education, makes this suggestion in *How Children Learn at Home*, which he co-authored with Harriet Pattison. Professor Thomas believes that in a modern industrial society children are surrounded by print: at home, in the street, in shops, on television, all over the place in fact. He finds it plausible that children could 'pick up' reading informally (Thomas and Pattison, 2007). He observes that some children educated in this way may not be able to read until the age of twelve or even older. Some believe that this does not matter and that once children do start to read, they soon catch up with those who learned to read at an earlier age.

Paul Goodman, in his book *Compulsory Miseducation* (1962), had this to say about learning to read:

> ...the puzzle is not how to teach reading, but why some children fail to learn to read. Given the amount of exposure that any urban child gets, any normal animal should spontaneously catch on to the code. What prevents? It is almost demonstrable that, for many children, it is precisely going to school that prevents – because of the school's alien style, banning of spontaneous interest, extrinsic rewards and punishments. (Goodman, 1962)

This neatly sums up what many autonomous educators believe: that schools are the cause of educational problems, not the solution.

There is an instinctive distaste for curricula among autonomous home educators, particularly for the National Curriculum. The expression, 'a

31

broad and balanced curriculum' is regarded as coercive mechanism for destroying the natural and wholesome curiosity of young children.

Autonomous home educators say that mathematics can be picked up in the same way as reading, as part of everyday life, rather than a dull academic subject found only in a textbook. They believe that by learning in this way, by seeing the relevance of the subject to ordinary, everyday life, the child will be more motivated and grasp at once the importance of mastering arithmetical concepts. History and geography too will be embedded in day to day life and so be seen as a natural part of affairs and not something only needed or delivered at school.

There is something in all this. Most of us are familiar with children for whom 'reading' is no more than a subject which they are forced to do at school. Such children would no more pick up a book for fun at home than they would try and solve a quadratic equation for their own amusement. Books and reading belong in school, along with history, mathematics and citizenship. Why would you want to do these things unless compelled to do so?

If done effectively, supervised by an enthusiastic adult ready to catch the child's interest and with appropriate resources readily at hand for when the child expresses a desire to learn of some topic, this system of autonomous learning at home might work. Such a home would be filled with books and other resources, and at least one adult who was devoted full time to providing learning opportunities and support for the child.

Learning to read naturally, by 'osmosis', is not a new idea. For some years it was a mainstream idea in schools. Using 'Real Books' enjoyed a vogue for a long time, the idea being that small children would be more attracted by real novels than by the traditional fare offered, such as *Peter and Jane* or *The Village with Three Corners*.

This approach has now been largely replaced in the UK by synthetic phonics: this is probably a better way of learning to read for most children than simply being handed a copy of *Treasure Island or Moonfleet*. David Bell, formerly Chief Inspector of Schools in England, delivered the pithiest judgement on this method of education when he referred to the, 'totally soft centred belief that children would learn if you left them to it,' as being 'Plain crackers' (Bell, 2004). A harsh judgement but one with which many people now agree.

It is also true, as autonomous educators point out, that child led, informal learning takes place in many homes up to the age of five. Suddenly, at this arbitrary age, it ends and is replaced with a structured curriculum. Nothing magical happens when a child reaches his fifth birthday which means that he should suddenly start learning in a completely different way. Some parents argue that all they are doing is to carry on that gentle, informal process into the child's later years.

We have talked so far about dedicated parents who are determined to allow their children to learn autonomously: these are intelligent mothers and fathers who believe in an unconventional educational philosophy. Unfortunately, not all parents who claim to be autonomous educators are like this.

Most local authority officers believe they know when they are dealing with a dedicated if eccentric educator. They may have reservations about the methods being used but as long as an education is being provided and they are convinced that the child's parents are committed to their child's learning they will generally not intervene. Such parents do not worry them. The problem is when the claim 'we're autonomous' is used to mask a lack of educational provision. Such cases cause grave concern.

Part of the judgement in the case of Iris Harrison, which we looked at in Chapter 1, reads as follows:

> In our judgement 'education' demands at least an element of supervision; merely to allow a child to follow its own devices in the hope that it will acquire knowledge by imitation, experiment or experience in its own way and in its own good time is neither systematic nor instructive ... such a course would not be education but, at best, childminding.' (*Harrison and Harrison v Stevenson*, 1982)

The possibility which alarms some of those charged with monitoring home education is that many parents are doing just this, leaving their children to their own devices in the hope that they will learn what is necessary under their own steam. As we see in the next chapter, autonomous education, however well conducted, can appear to the outsider as no education at all. This may be why so many autonomously educating parents are reluctant to allow visits.

However the suspicion remains that there are parents who under the guise of autonomous education are not actually providing an education for their child. It is common on Internet support groups for home educators to see parents who have just withdrawn their children from school asking, 'what shall we do now?' It is plain that they have removed their children from school in response to some crisis and have no idea of what to do next. For such parents, autonomous education with its lack of structure and planning, must seem like an ideal solution. Some seem to think that there is no need to do anything: the child is in charge of her learning and if she decides to sit and watch television all day, we must respect her decision. Who's to say that this is any less valuable than reading Dickens?

Even more worrying is some of the advice given to such parents. Some claim that after being in the school system, children need to be detoxified by spending a period of time just laying around doing nothing before they commence anything educational. This is known as 'de-schooling' and the standard recommendation is that children should spend a month for each year they have been in school, doing absolutely nothing. So a teenager who was de-registered at the age of fourteen, in the run up to his GCSEs, might be advised to spend the best part of a year doing nothing but watching television and taking it easy. No wonder local authority officers are concerned.

The final category of those who have chosen home education as a positive route rather than in response to some difficulty, are parents who do not wish their children to attend school for cultural or religious reasons. There is some unease about this because a child could end up being indoctrinated with her parents' religious views and this might create later difficulties integrating into wider society. It appears that many of those who undertake the education of their children for religious reasons tend to be quite structured in their approach. Jehovah's Witnesses and Plymouth Brethren are both Christian denominations which are known to favour home education, more to preserve the child from contamination by a godless society, than because it is felt that the quality of education offered by schools is lacking or inferior. Sometimes such parents object to the teaching of evolution or morality by schools and would rather handle these topics in their own way, in accordance with their beliefs.

Some Christian home educators use educational resources from America which manage to introduce a Christian perspective to every academic subject. Many local authority officers enjoy monitoring visits to such families. The children are polite and the parents are definitely teaching them. They are unlikely to go to a religious household and find the kids slumped in front of a computer, playing Grand Theft Auto IV.

Anecdotal evidence from Internet lists like HE-UK and Education Otherwise suggest that a fair number of Muslims are also choosing to educate their children at home for religious and cultural reasons. One concern here, as with Christians and Jews who are doing so, is that religious instruction might tend to dominate over traditional subjects such as history, science and geography. It is debateable whether this should be any business of the local authority and, as long as an education *is* provided, it is generally felt wisest to leave it at that.

The Gypsy/Roma/Traveller community are another group who sometimes decide that they do not wish their children to be educated in schools. This is usually because they believe that the education being offered at school will not be particularly helpful to their children for the lifestyle they are likely to lead (Ivatts, 2006). This is a tricky issue. As long ago as 1985, this question was debated in the courts with reference to a Jewish school. It was decided that a suitable education in law was one which:

> Primarily equips a child for life within the community of which he is a member, rather than the way of life in the country as a whole, as long as it does not foreclose the child's options in later years to adopt some other form of life if he wishes to do so. (Woolf, 1985)

This judgement clearly has wide ranging implications not only for the Gypsy/Roma/Traveller community, but also for Muslims, Christians, Jews and others who choose to educate their own children for religious or cultural reasons. What of a child who was brought up in an Arabic or Yiddish speaking household and did not learn English? Or a culture where it was felt that the education of girls should cease at puberty? There are no definitive answers to these questions and they are decided on a case by case basis.

There is a suspicion that the value of education after the age of twelve or thirteen is not always appreciated by the Gypsy/Roma/Traveller community. Clearly, if the adults of any community have flourished without academic study, they may tend to see studying as less important than learning how to live and take their place within the community of which they are members (Ivatts, 2006).

Home education, then, can engender tensions between local authorities and parents. Some of these are rooted in parents' feelings of injustice and being failed by the system. Others are due to the belief by local authority officers that some of the children they see being withdrawn from school are not receiving a suitable education at home. There is, however, a wider unease among local authorities and also in the government.

Until thirty years ago the number of parents teaching their own children was tiny. They were a handful of cranks and enthusiasts, the fanatical home educators like Harry Lawrence and the laid back types such as Iris Harrison. As long as the practice of home education was restricted to a few dozen mavericks and eccentrics, the phenomenon was not really a problem. But we are no longer talking about a couple of dozen children: home education has become a mass movement, with tens of thousands of children being educated out of school. It is this development which has prompted a change in the law and a demand for increased regulation.

Our history provides many examples of activities which are tolerated to a greater or lesser degree while only a few individuals are involved. Driving motor cars on public roads is one instance, the consumption of cannabis is another. When the numbers of people involved in these things reaches a certain level, the state steps in and regulates or sometimes prohibits the activity. The number of children who are not being sent to school continues to rise steadily and at this rate it will soon reach the hundred thousand mark. In the USA anywhere between one and two million children are currently home educated. There are differences between home education in America and Britain but one of the greatest is that of the primary motivation behind the enterprise. In Chapter 4 we explore the research on home education in these two countries but here we consider the question of motivation.

The National Centre for Education Statistics in America carried out a large survey a few years ago, looking at the motivation for home education. Almost 50 per cent of parents gave as their main reason, 'Can give child a better education at home' (US Department of Education, 1999). When Paula Rothermel of Durham University analysed what home education meant to home educators, the result was somewhat different. In *The Third Way in Education* (2000), Dr. Rothermel revealed that what mattered most to British parents about home education was: 'having a close family relationship and being together' and 'having the freedom and flexibility to do what we want, when we want' (Rothermel, 2000). So the main attraction of home education had nothing to do with education! This was a surprising discovery: home education was more a lifestyle choice than a desire to educate as such.

This research took place over twelve years ago, chiefly among those belonging to the support group Education Otherwise. Things may well have changed since then, although Thomas and Pattison (2007) recently found the same attitude still prevailed. If it were true that American parents tend to home educate because of their concern for education and that British parents do so for reasons unconnected with education, it might explain why in 2009 the DCSF seemed determined to bring home education under some sort of control.

There is in reality no such thing as 'Home Educators' or the 'home educating community'. There are tens of thousands of parents, each with their own motives for being home educators and with widely differing opinions on the best way of going about it. Many who wish to investigate it turn to the large organisations so that they can get a handle on the practice of home education.

They may join organisations like Education Otherwise or Home Education UK when they first make the decision to teach their own children. Many allow their membership to lapse after the first year or so. Even those who carry on paying their yearly subscription usually do so because membership enables them to keep in touch with other home educators and find out what is happening on the home education scene, rather than because they wish to become actively involved. So while a support group like Education Otherwise might nominally have three thousand members, only a handful are active in shaping the policy of the organisation and formulating a response to research. The same is true of other such groups: The public voice of such organisations might not be representative of all its members.

When newspapers carry bold headlines claiming that 'Home Educators Reject Government Plans' or 'Home Educating Parents Up In Arms' this can mean no more than that one or two individuals from a single group have written a press release or telephoned a newspaper. For example soon after the Badman review was announced, the BBC carried a piece headlined, 'home educators are angry at review'. Careful reading revealed that only one parent was angry, a spokeswoman for Education Otherwise (BBC, 2009). It does not mean that all or even most home educators share this view, as became clear during this review of home education and the run-up to the meetings of the commons select committee which looked into the conduct of the review.

Three home education groups co-ordinated campaigns against the review and, via online communities, made sure that several hundred responses were made, almost all of them rejecting the underlying rationale behind the review. These were Home Education UK, Education Otherwise plus an Internet list set up specifically to combat the review; the Badman Review Action Group. Sometimes each member of a family would send a separate response to boost the numbers, and one woman sent three responses (CSF select committee report, 2009). Many of those who objected were not actually home educators. The two or three hundred parents who expressed strong views against the recommendations made by Graham Badman in his report on home education thus represented a tiny proportion of home educators. We have no idea what the vast majority think about the matter.

The more militant autonomous educators are well organised and give the impression of being far more numerous than they are. A core of activists patrol the Internet looking for debates about home education taking place online. Should a newspaper or magazine run a piece on home education and it is possible to post comments online, the comments section will at once be flooded with pro home education posts (eg *TES*, *Independent*, 2009). Anybody who is critical of home education will be challenged. The same names can be seen again and again. One mother living in Surrey posts comments on articles on home education in local newspapers as far afield as Lancashire and Portsmouth.

The DCSF announced in November 2009 that they would no longer respond to Freedom of Information requests from certain autonomous home educators. After the publication of the Badman Report, they had received hundreds of FOI requests. The DCSF revealed that 70 per cent of this huge number came from nine individuals, all well known in home educating circles. The DCSF had already declined to give some information because of a vicious campaign which was being waged against Graham Badman and his family on the Internet.

Watching the struggle against any change in the *status quo* of British home education one might get a picture of a small band of determined activists who see themselves as the shock troops of the home education movement, fighting for all home educators.

To some extent home education in the UK can be said to be a victim of its own success. With so many children now being withdrawn from school, it is no longer possible for professionals in the field of education to dismiss it as a fringe activity: it is plainly here to stay.

But largely because of the advice given to new home educators by certain home education support groups and in online communities these groups are the architects of their own misfortune: such advice has led to local authorities making demands for new powers.

As the law has stood for many years, parents educating their children at home are not obliged to allow anybody into their homes to check on the provision being made. As we have seen, the local authorities may make informal enquiries and parents are well advised to respond. More and more are limiting their information to Educational Philosophies downloaded from various websites. When parents ask on online forums what they should expect in dealings with Education Welfare Officers or other representatives of the local authority, they are frequently advised to have nothing to do with them. They are provided with the relevant legal precedents and encouraged to refuse to allow anybody from the local authority near them or their children. This tends to create a mindset of resistance in some parents, who have been made to feel they are being persecuted by unsympathetic officialdom and may already be ill disposed towards anybody from the local authority, for reasons discussed earlier.

However, if local authorities cannot see the children who are home educated, how can they establish that the children are safe, well and being educated to an acceptable standard (Badman Report, 2009; CSF select committee, 2009)? Therefore the local authorities who submitted evidence to the Badman review were unanimous in wanting new and increased powers to enable them to fulfill their duties, both in monitoring education and in ensuring that the children in their area were safe and well.

A dramatic case is made through the tragedy of Khyra Ishaq, the little girl who starved to death after she was taken out of school by her mother. Khyra's mother refused to allow Educational Welfare Officers or social workers into her home and sometimes refused to answer the door. As the law stands, she was within her rights to do so. Five months after the child had been withdrawn from school she was dead. Although rare, it is cases like this which make local authorities want extra powers to intervene if they have suspicions that all is not well in a household where home education is being undertaken.

The shake-up which is currently engulfing home education should be a good thing in the end. It has certainly made both local authorities and home educating parents think deeply about what they are doing and what they hope to achieve.

Shortly before this book went to press, there were two further developments. Ofsted released the results of the study of home education which they conducted in 2009 (discussed in Chapter 4). The main point was that Ofsted called for the same compulsory registration of home educators as Badman had done a year earlier. The second development is a result of the change of government. Michael Gove, the new Education Secretary, announced that the coalition would encourage the setting up of so-called free schools of the kind found in Sweden. As we saw in Chapter 1, such free schools had been set up by home educating parents as long ago as the early 1970s. Unfortunately Gove recommended the Swedish model of education in the same month that the Swedish parliament approved a law to ban home education and impose a state sponsored curriculum in all the free schools, which had ben found inadequate.

Few home educators seem to be enthusiastic about the idea of small, independent schools set up and run by parents. They see two problems. Firstly, they fear that if parents who are unhappy with maintained schools set up free schools, this would reduce the number of home educators, possibly to the level where so few are involved that a future government might feel able to ban the practice entirely, as happened in Sweden. Secondly, there would be nothing to stop the government imposing the National Curriculum upon these free schools, as Sweden has now done.

However, parents home educate because they want to educate their children at home and not send them to school. Consequently, any new type of school is likely to be irrelevant to them. On a practical level, any new free school will first have to demonstrate a local demand, with at least forty parents involved. Home educating families are scattered over wide geographical areas and are unlikely to fulfil this requirement. Consequently, this initiative is unlikely to affect most home educating families.

3

Who are the home educators and what do they do?

Schools and their influence permeate the lives of parents to such an extent that most are unaware of it. They are so used to the school run, the open evening, the sports day and the nativity play that they find it inconceivable that a parent with young children or teenagers would not be involved in this world (Durbin, 2009). Often support networks and social lives are built into this lifestyle. The exchanges at the school gates, the invitations to parties, arrangements for play-dates and so on are regarded as being the norm for any parent with a young child of school age. The situation is very different for the parent who decides to educate her own child.

Home education is not just another way of teaching children; it entails a radically different lifestyle from most other families'. It can attract opprobrium from those with whom the home educating parent comes into contact: from the woman at the supermarket checkout to the doctor's receptionist. The simple enquiry to a child of: 'no school today?' can become immensely irritating for the accompanying parent, when heard day in, day out for years. Even worse than irritation can be encountering the hostility when they reveal that their children do not attend school and that it is not a question of 'no school today' but of 'no school any day'.

Until it is understood that home education involves a completely different lifestyle, it will be hard for anybody who is not part of this community to put themselves in the place of the mother or father with a child who does not attend school. Many parents in this position already feel a little beleaguered: they are aware that they have made a choice which sets them apart from other parents. This might make them unduly sensitive to any sort of implied criticism of their lifestyle.

Local education officers and teachers often find it staggering that ordinary parents feel they can provide their children with an education of anything like the quality of what is routinely provided by highly trained staff working in purpose built establishments equipped with specialised resources such as laboratories, music rooms and gymnasia. During Badman's review of home education the National Association of Schoolmasters/Union of Women teachers said:

> The NASUWT maintains the existence of a right to home educate is anomalous with the clear emphasis in Government policy of ensuring that all children and young people can benefit from educational provision where teaching and learning is led by qualified teachers in well resourced and fit for purpose modern educational settings. (Badman, 2009)

No parent in an ordinary household can compete with a school in providing the facilities for modern education. However, it is perfectly possible to teach any academic subject efficiently at home. Working closely to the subject specification, easily downloaded from the Internet, parents can and do teach their children any and every subject. With a little ingenuity and improvisation, chemistry experiments can be conducted in the kitchen with materials bought from a supermarket. It is certainly easier to use a Bunsen burner than a ring on the gas cooker, but it is not essential to the learning of the principles of chemistry (Webb, 1990). The same can be said of music, history, English and any other subject. It is hard work, but it can be done. It is by no means uncommon for children taught at home to obtain good passes at GCSE, or International GCSE. It is important to remember that historically, education took place in just this way, with a parent instructing a child without any of the paraphernalia of modern schools. Laboratories, electronic whiteboards, laser pointers, sports fields and gymnasia are useful aids when teaching thirty children, but wholly unnecessary for the instruction of a single child.

At this point I abandon objectivity to give a brief personal account of how academic standards can be maintained outside the modern, fit for purpose educational settings of which the teaching unions are rightly proud. This can be and is accomplished regularly by home educators: that academic excellence need not be restricted to purpose built institutions staffed by qualified teachers.

My daughter passed eight International GCSEs, all at A*. The subjects taken were: physics, chemistry, biology, mathematics, history, English language, English literature and religious studies. In addition to this she achieved Grade 6 (Bronze Medal) Acting with LAMDA and Grade 5 ABRSM Guitar. She represented her county at chess tournaments and has won trophies for fencing. This child did not spend a single day in school and was taught only by her parents. Nor is she an exceptional case. Children are often taught outside school by unqualified parents and some achieve remarkable results academically.

However, what many home educating parents mean by 'education' is not what most teachers would understand by the word. So while it is perfectly possible to teach any academic subject at the kitchen table, many parents would not even attempt to do so unless their children had specifically asked to be taught. For these autonomously educating parents the lack of specialised provision is not so much a handicap as an irrelevance.

Autonomous education is a form of Inquiry-based Learning, in which the initiative to learn comes from the child. It is the child who chooses what to study and how extensive her studies will be. Their parents have, as a matter of principle, no intention of providing their children with a broad and balanced curriculum. That is not to say that they refuse to teach their children about physics and chemistry or history and geography – but that they will not do so as a matter of course: the impetus must come from the child. We looked in the last chapter at the theoretical underpinning for these practices. This chapter considers how they work in action.

Parents who follow the path of autonomous education vary greatly in the degree of autonomy which they are prepared to grant to their children. Some oppose even the teaching of reading to young children, believing that they will somehow pick it up automatically, simply by virtue of being exposed to the printed words which surround us in our society (Thomas and Pattison, 2007). Such parents may also allow their children to decide bedtimes, diet and whether they clean their teeth. Sometimes no limit is set upon the amount of time children are allowed to watch television or play computer games during the day. It is claimed that young children will learn to read from the instructions in computer games and that because this is information which they actually want to acquire, it will motivate their learning in a way that reading a specially designed reading book will not. This ties in with what we saw earlier of Karl Popper's philosophy and the idea of intrinsic and extrinsic learning.

With no set bedtimes and no need to get up for school in the mornings, these households might seem chaotic and unstructured, with no teaching and apparently little learning taking place. A local authority officer tells of visiting a home educating family at 11 am and finding the child still in pyjamas and slumped in front of a television watching an adult programme. However some researchers support such freedom.

Professor Alan Thomas, for example, a respected psychologist, has carried out a good deal of research into home education in the UK and Australia. In his work with home educating families, Professor Thomas says he has found that when they first decide to home educate, parents try to reproduce the school environment at home. Most drop this approach after a short while and adopt a more relaxed and informal style, with the child learning in the course of conversations and everyday activities. Thomas maintains that this 'informal learning' is no less effective than conventional teaching (Thomas and Pattison, 2007). It takes place all the time when children are small, right up until they start school. At this point it stops abruptly for many children and is replaced with a curriculum delivered in a highly structured institutional setting. Many home educating parents question why this should be so. Because if this style of learning works well up to the age of five, is there any reason to suppose that it cannot continue to work with older children?

Home educating parents sometimes seem defensive about their methods, especially if the local authority charged with monitoring their home education expects to see curricula and plans for taking GCSEs. Parents receiving visits from these authorities suspect they are being judged according to school standards or are even seen to be neglecting their children. Some local authority officers are certainly anxious, because they feel that these children are not receiving an education. However parents point out that when their children do become interested in a topic, they pursue it for weeks or months at a time.

Much of the tension between local authorities and home educating parents concerns parents who are not planning their children's education and are failing to provide tuition in a structured and systematic way. Local authority officers have a problem with a particular kind of home education rather than home educators as such. It is hard to see how there can be a resolution to these conflicts (although Chapter 7 offers a model for home education practice which might satisfy both sides). Even a request for an outline of what direction the child's education might take in the course of the next twelve months has proved an insuperable stumbling block when dealing with many home educators (Children, Schools and Families select committee, 2009).

Given that their children are in control of their own education and decide what they learn and when and how they learn it, how could a plan for the coming year even be considered? Some parents claim that this requirement alone would, if implemented, render their own favoured style of education impossible. It has been seriously compared to the situation with a quantum system; the act of examining or measuring it irrevocably changes what is being measured.

Local authority officers find parents who follow a more structured approach to their children's education far easier to deal with but then they are usually people who have a conventional approach to education. And structured home education is an astonishingly effective way of teaching. Let us look at how this type of education works in practice.

Teaching at home is an entirely different matter from teaching in a school. Teaching in a school typically entails the supervision of thirty or so youngsters, some of whom may be disruptive, reluctant to learn or have various special needs. In the course of the few hours a week allocated for each subject, this disparate group must be led, goaded and cajoled into behaving properly and grasping the rudiments of whatever topic is being tackled. Set against this is practically unlimited one to one tuition in a relaxed domestic setting. It is not surprising that children can make rapid academic progress under these conditions.

A great deal of a primary school pupil's time at school is spent just waiting. Waiting for the others to settle down, waiting for the attention of the teacher, waiting for some children to stop mucking about: the actual teaching time in the average day probably does not amount to more than a couple of hours. This is why many structured home educators tend to work hard in the morning for two or three hours and leave the afternoons free for outings and activities. During the specified hours though, the child is actually working; there is no waiting time. Any point about which the child is unclear can be dealt with immediately, questions are answered at once, the books required are close at hand, the whole teaching process is intensive, with no interruptions. One could describe it as an individualised learning plan.

Children taught in this way make fast progress. There has been little research on home education in the UK, but research from America is encouraging and strongly suggests that those home educated children who are actually being taught achieve better academically than their schooled peers (Ray, 2003; Rudner, 1999).

In addition to the time spent studying at the kitchen table, the home educated child has more opportunity for extra-mural visits and excursions (Farris, 1997). Not for many home educators the once a term trip to the museum! If the topic being studied is, say, World War II, a whole raft of visits can take place to bring the subject to life. For those who live in or near London, this might include trips to HMS Belfast moored in the Thames, the Imperial War Museum, the Cabinet War rooms in Whitehall and the Churchill museum attached to them, the National Army Museum, a day out to the Royal Dockyards at Chatham, visiting an elderly relative who actually fought in World War II ... the list is endless.

Sometimes, groups of home educating parents band together and arrange to teach their children in something more approaching a classroom setting, albeit a relaxed and informal one. This sort of activity also provides social opportunities for the children.

Throughout the day, the same kind of informal learning by conversation that we saw as a feature of autonomous education is taking place, in addition to the structured teaching. One of the first things people meeting home educated teenagers notice is that they tend to be articulate and unafraid to express their views and opinions. This is hardly surprising since they spend their days in the company of adults rather than other children: an almost inevitable feature of home education, whether structured or autonomous.

One of the commonest myths about home educated children (discussed in Chapter 6) is that they might lack socialisation and be shy and withdrawn. The archetypal home educated child in the public consciousness is probably a pale, precocious, socially inept and studious child. Such children do exist but they are the exception rather than the rule. When asked whether she thought her daughter would benefit from socialising with other children, one mother who had withdrawn her child from school remarked bitterly: 'I can teach my daughter to burp, fart, spit, swear, smoke and drink just as well as anyone else can.'

Two major styles or trends in home education, structured and autonomous, have been compared and contrasted as though they were opposites. In reality the two methods overlap and merge. No home educating parent is so fanatically structured that no autonomy exists, just as the most dedicated autonomously educating parent imposes at least some structure on her child's learning. Some parents, for example, insist upon teaching their children the rudiments of reading and writing, then allow them free choice about what they want to learn about after that. Others have a fairly structured approach but with plenty of scope for wandering down the byways of study and spending a long time on some obscure topic which interests the child.

For both structured and autonomously educating parents, the school day and the school year are an irrelevance. Learning does not begin at a particular time of day, nor end promptly at four o'clock. An autonomously educated child who is engrossed with some project can be working on it under his own steam late into the night. School holidays may see a change of pace but only because the child might have friends who attend school and cannot otherwise be seen on weekday mornings.

This is one of the great advantages of home education: that an interest can be pursued at length while the child's enthusiasm is strong. For instance, if during the study of history the child expresses the wish to see a castle, an expedition can be planned for the following day. The mathematics which had been planned for that day can easily be post-poned and the next few days spent on history and little else. This style of teaching, of striking while the iron is hot, is common to most home educators. It would be hard to find a home educating parent who adhered so rigidly to a timetable or curriculum that he was unwilling to launch into spontaneous learning of this sort. Spontaneity of this kind is impossible in schools, where every excursion must be planned well in advance and the interests of thirty children must be considered, rather than one or two.

The advent of the Internet has been a tremendous boon for home edu-cators. In addition to the support provided for parents by online com-munities and various groups (see Chapter 2), there is practically unlimited academic material available. Apart from the more obvious resources such as various online encyclopaedias, it is possible to down-load the entire National Curriculum and the specifications for almost any GCSE or A level. It is entirely feasible for a parent to educate a child from primary level to A levels by relying wholly upon teaching resources to be found free on the Internet – although few depend entirely on the Internet for learning.

There are also a number of Internet 'schools' where children can be members of an online community which mimics the school environ-ment, even including the chance to chat during breaks. Some children study for GCSEs in this way, using distance learning providers.

There is no way of knowing how many home educated children sit formal examinations such as GCSEs. Quite a few parents who favour this path tend to opt instead for the International GCSE or (IGCSE). There are excellent reasons for this. In the first place, the IGCSE may be taken purely as an examination, rather in the fashion of the old O level GCE. This obviates the need for the marking of coursework, something of a problem for home educating parents. Even the phasing out of coursework in favour of work carried out under controlled conditions in the classroom is unlikely to make the GCSE any more attractive to home educators.

Another great advantage of the IGCSE is that it is regarded more highly by many employers, colleges and universities. Although nominally equivalent to GCSEs, many believe the IGCSE to be more rigorous and a better indication of academic achievement. As has already been mentioned, taking GCSEs or IGCSEs is an expensive and time consuming process, which might explain why not all home educated children take them. Few schools or colleges welcome external candidates and tracking down a suitable school or college can be a frustrating experience.

Understandably, most schools do not encourage private candidates. The whole process of entering children for GCSEs in a school is a smooth and well oiled production line. Fifty for this subject, two hundred for that. The teacher knows who will be taking Higher Tier and who Foundation. Everybody knows their part. The home educating parent, on the other hand, can be labour intensive. She must be instructed in all the details which the school staff take for granted and will probably ring the school with additional questions half a dozen times. This is to say nothing of requests for extra time, scribes or a separate, quiet room. One of Badman's recommendations was that local authorities should make exam centres available for home educated children and also should pay for their entries. If implemented, this recommendation would greatly help home educated children who sit GCSEs.

Some Christian parents use the Accelerated Christian Education material. This is a course of highly structured material which can ultimately lead to a qualification which is in theory equivalent to GCSEs and A levels. Other children study with the Open University from the age of fourteen or fifteen: sometimes much younger. Some parents get their teenage children to take the National Tests in Adult Literacy and Numeracy. Level 2 of these tests is supposedly the equivalent to a GCSE at Grades A*-C. The aim in many cases is to enable them to gain entry to college or university without taking GCSEs or A levels.

The problem is the myth that exists among home educating parents that a child can get a place at college or university without taking any GCSEs or A levels. But this is not as easy as parents think. On home education Internet message boards, parents often talk of the possibility of their child applying for some course by putting together a portfolio of work. This might just work if the subject is photography, textiles or media studies, but for a child wishing to study A levels, it will not do. Many Further Education Colleges are now adamant that those wishing to study for A levels need to have already taken GCSEs in the subject.

The disinclination of many parents to encourage their children to study systematically for formal qualifications can profoundly affect their life chances.

Few colleges now offer the chance to study or take GCSEs, except as re-sits, so parents who have not made private arrangements discover that their children will have to make do without these qualifications. As a result, some colleges and universities find themselves presented with a home educated teenager applying for a place, who boasts only a few Level 2 National Tests in Literacy and a couple of units of an Open University course. In general, they prefer to play safe and accept students with the usual five GCSEs and three A levels.

The two big 'spikes' in de-registering children from school come soon after they start school and again when the change to secondary school is made. Local authority officers are increasingly speaking of an additional, third 'spike'. This takes place at around the age of fourteen, when the children are beginning to study intensively for their GCSEs (CSF select committee, 2009). This is the age at which some teenagers become disaffected and drop out of school. This has nothing to do with home education *per se* but it is by no means impossible that some parents at this stage de-register their children from school, supposedly so that they can be taught at home while actually trying to avoid trouble both with their teenage children and also their local authority.

One reason that parents and children seem to get on so well in families who home educate is that the children are not spending all day with other children. They are not constantly being encouraged to demand a particular brand of trainer or make of mobile telephone; they do not have to have the latest 'must have' toy or game; their conversation is usually about other topics than who won The X Factor. Home educated children are generally more self directed than schooled children and tend to make far fewer demands for items driven by fashion than is true among their peer group who attend school.

The close relationship which many home educated children have with their parents can have disadvantages, however. Children learning at home tend to argue less with their parents, yet tensions between parents and children which sometimes turn into rows can have a positive side. Arguably, such friction is often initiated by the child herself, as she tries to assert her independence from her mother and father. The cause of the rows is largely irrelevant: they can be sparked off over the most trivial issues. The point is that they show a child struggling to come to terms with the fact that she is an independent human being with a mind of her own and has wishes of her own which conflict with the desires of her parents. She is seeking to break free – and this is a healthy and necessary part of growing up.

Home educated children strike some observers as being unnaturally close to their parents. They seem less prone to shouting and tantrums. Many of them speak in an eerily adult way, using complex vocabulary and figures of speech well above their chronological age. At times they hardly appear to be children at all (Walmsley and Margolis, 1987). This may be an inevitable consequence of spending a lot of time in the company of adults and may not in itself be a bad thing. However, this closeness might sometimes make it hard for the child to assert his right to independence: he may behave more like an adult partner than a little boy. It is sometimes suggested that such children are in some way fulfilling the parents' need for a sympathetic companion and not a rebellious child.

The mothers and fathers of teenagers attending school may be jealous of the close relationships which many home educating parents have with their offspring. There is certainly a good deal of historical evidence which suggests that the whole teenage rebellion business is a recent and freakish trend (Neufeld and Mate, 2004). So the cordial relations enjoyed by many home educating parents with their adolescent children might be normal and the friction and conflicts so common in homes where the children have attended school might themselves be the aberration!

It is impossible to generalise about home educating parents and their methods; there is no such thing as a 'typical' home educator. Instead, there is a spectrum of methods, made up of thousands of individual parents, each with their own individual way of working. Their techniques range from affording the child a degree of autonomy which verges on neglect, to a level of structure and supervision which is so unrelenting as to appear cruel. In between these extremes are the great mass of home educating parents, doing the best they can for their children. And all enjoy the company of their children.

Home educating parents avoid the anxiety of packing their two year-olds off to nursery. Not for them the groans of dismay at the prospect of having their child on their hands during the summer holidays. They *like* their children and enjoy their company. The more they see of them the better. This definitely marks home educators out as being unusual. Perhaps it is this pleasure of parents in the company of their own children which makes some people uneasy about home education. It may seem unnatural to many that a parent would want to have a toddler or teenager around the house for twenty four hours a day. It is possible that this feeling that there is something too close about the relationship which home educated children typically have with their parents which leads to the suggestion that home educated children are at greater risk of being abused. This idea seems constantly to lurk on the edge of debates about home education, as we shall see in Chapter 6. But first we examine the research on elective home education.

4

The research on home education

Relatively little research has been carried out on home education in Britain. What there is is often based upon absurdly small, self-selected samples (Rothermel, 2002; Thomas and Pattison, 2007). Those seeking to justify or criticise British home education may be compelled to fall back upon American research, although the American and British models of home education may not be similar enough to make comparisons valid.

The one piece of research which is quoted in any discussion of home education in the UK is that conducted by Paula Rothermel, a student at Durham University. She sent out 2500 questionnaires to home educators who were members of Education Otherwise. The following year she sent out the same number again and a small number to Local Education Authorities and elsewhere. This work was carried out as part of her studies and subsequently formed the subject of her PhD thesis. Rothermel received over a thousand responses. She investigated a little over 400 of them in depth. From all this emerged a number of fairly dramatic claims, not all of them made by Rothermel herself. But they have nevertheless become part of the mythology associated with this survey and are still quoted uncritically.

One claim was that home educated children scored significantly higher on standard tests of literacy than children of similar age at school. Using the assessments for literacy which Rothermel did, one would expect to find 16 per cent of children in the top band. According to Rothermel, 94 per cent of home educated six year olds were in this band (Rothermel,

1998). Academically, the home educated children were generally well in advance of schooled children in most areas. Another claim is that this work demonstrated that working-class children who were home educated did better than middle-class children (Rothermel, 1998). These are extraordinary claims, so how were such conclusions reached?

The conclusions about educational attainment were not drawn from examining the thousand questionnaires returned. Nor were they the result of analysing the sample of 419 responses that were examined in detail. It was the literacy tests applied to 67 children which were the grounds for some of the most remarkable findings. Furthermore, these tests were not conducted under controlled conditions by the researcher herself but were posted out to parents with instructions about how to go about administering them. Only five children were subsequently re-tested by Rothermel herself (Rothermel, 2002).

The methods invited problems. In some cases the tests were left lying around the house for some time: one mother apologised for the sticky marks on the paper because it had been left in the kitchen. It is impossible to know if the children were prompted, whether siblings helped, if the children saw the tests for some time before they were administered or even if the test results were actually those of the home educated children in the study. It is easy to imagine an eager parent showing an uncomprehending child a word and then saying irritably, 'Come on, you do know that word. Look, it begins with a C!' The tests might have been conducted more than once and so, in effect, the children were coached to achieve high results.

Thus all but the five tests Rothermel carried out under controlled conditions can be discarded as unreliable and there are even questions about those five. Were the tests upon which the children were re-tested identical to those which they had already taken? If so, might the initial testing and seeing the papers round the house have had the effect of teaching these children the correct answers?

Rothermel also administered other academic tests in person. They were PIPS; Performance Indicators in Primary Schools assessments. Thirty five of these were carried out. So her own testing amounted to 35 families tested through PIPS and five children to whom she administered the NLS literacy tests to measure the educational attainment of home educated children. Yet this small sample is widely cited by advocates of home education in Britain.

When dealing with a self-selected sample, we need to ask who might participate in such research. Is it more likely to be those who feel confident about what they are doing? Were the respondents typical of home educating families in general? Significantly, 95 per cent of the questionnaires were sent to Education Otherwise members. Is the picture of academic attainment different for those who are not members of Education Otherwise nor registered with their local authority? Rothermel herself was aware of the limitations of the exercise, stating that 'This report should be taken for what it is, an exploratory window on home-education' (Rothermel, 2002).

It was also claimed that Rothermel's research showed that working-class children thrived under the regimen of home education, outstripping middle-class children (*TES*, 1999). This echoes the assertion made by researchers in the United States that home educated black children do better than those at school (Ray, 1997). But colour is easier to define than what we mean by 'working-class'. Questions of class and income are difficult to identify with any precision. Moreover, these matters of class, income, career and education were all self-allocated by those who completed the questionnaires and who may have had their own agenda.

Reliable research on home education is certainly needed. When we are considering a child's education, the first thing we should ask is, 'Does it work?' or at least, 'Does it work a lot of the time?' But many home educating parents resist the idea of research and are suspicious about the idea of trying to gather reliable data about home education. And it is vital that it cover a large number of children. A large sample will even out any statistical flukes and give us a reliable picture of what approaches are effective in home education.

Since the time of the ancient Babylonians, it has been assumed that children need to be actively taught to read and write and there is much evidence to substantiate this view. However, in the last few decades the idea has gained some currency that children can and will teach themselves. This is variously described as autonomous learning, unschooling, natural learning and child-led education. Parents reading books by educationalists such as Alan Thomas might be led to believe that the development of literacy and numeracy is a simple process which can happen automatically to their children (Thomas and Pattison, 2007). Recently poplar books published about home education could similarly mislead (Durbin, 2009; Mountney, 2009). Because of the lack of empirical research, parents who are considering home educating their children often turn to online communities for advice. Some will advocate that they need not instruct their children in reading or arithmetic but that they will acquire both literacy and numeracy naturally, just as they learned to speak.

Alan Thomas studied home educated families and published his findings in several books, notably *Educating Your Child at Home* (2002), written with Jane Lowe and *How Children Learn at Home* (2008), with Harriet Pattinson.

In *How Children Learn at Home*, Thomas and Pattison look in detail at 26 families, mostly English, but including a few Australian, Irish and Canadian families. In previous work, Thomas had found that although many home educating parents initially began teaching their children in a structured way, almost without exception they stopped doing so after a while and began teaching in a more informal way. *How Children Learn at Home* explores this informal learning in great detail, through extensive, open-ended interviews with the families taking part in his project. He and Harriet Pattinson, herself a home educating parent with a background in social anthropology, make the point that not only do young children learn a great deal informally with their parents before they start school, but that older children in societies where school is not the custom continue to learn as part of everyday life with the adults with whom they spend their days.

In addition to what they described as the 'Everyday Cultural Curriculum', or learning about day to day life, Thomas and Pattinson found that children educated in this way learned a great deal by asking questions, mainly of their parents (Thomas and Pattinson, 2008). There was no direction to this style of learning, apart from the child's interest, but it went on continually. An interesting contrast concerned questions. With home education, it is children who ask most of the questions as they seek information about the world around them. In schools the opposite is true: the adults ask most of the questions. Another difference is that when a child asks a question, it is usually because she genuinely wishes to know the answer: she is asking because she does not know something she wishes to know. In schools the adults asking the questions already know the answers and are simply testing the knowledge of the children.

Other recent research was the survey by Education Otherwise of all its members in 2003. In 2006 the National Foundation for Educational Research published *Some Perspectives on Home Educated Children.* Also in 2006, York Consulting conducted a study for the Department of Education and Science, *The Prevalence of Home education in England: A Feasibility Study* (2007). All three studies found that the main reason why parents decided to home educate was their dissatisfaction with schools' inability to deal with children's problems.

For their survey, Education Otherwise distributed 2500 questionnaires to members, a fifth of whom responded. So again the responses were self-selected. Of those who had de-registered their children from school, the commonest reasons for doing so were bullying and school phobia. Respondents could give more than one answer to questions and overall about a third said that the strongest influences on their decision to home educate were related to family lifestyle.

Much the same picture emerged from the York Consulting study, with similar reasons given for the decision to home educate. Some home educators have criticised the work by York Consulting because it covered only nine local authority areas, three of which had a disproportionately large number of Gypsy/Roma/Traveller home educators (Hopwood *et al*, 2007). In one local authority, two thirds of home educating parents known to the local authority came from this group.

In June 2010 Ofsted published the results of the survey which they conducted at the end of 2009, *Local authorities and home education* (Ofsted, 2010). It outlined research into fifteen local authorities. Local authority officers and home educating parents were interviewed, along with over a hundred home educated children and young people.

Thus there is no study which takes a large group of all home educating families in one area and analyses each one. The samples in the research in this field are all skewed and biased in one way or another.

Even the respected and longstanding Education Otherwise found that 80 per cent of their own members did not wish to take part in their study of what home educating parents thought and felt. York Consulting, too, observed that the questionnaires which were distributed for them by home education groups elicited a poor response. To see large scale, meticulous research, we must turn to the United States but this raises a serious question.

We have seen that in America the primary motive for home education is that parents feel they can provide a better education for their children than that offered at the local school. But another widespread motivation – which may run alongside wishing to provide a good education – is religious belief. So widespread is this reason for home education that American home educators are often characterised as belonging predominantly to the Christian Right. Parents who keep their children away from schools because they feel that schools are godless places incapable of providing a decent education will have different views from those who choose autonomous education for social and educational reasons. This has implications for the relevance to the UK of the American research.

Before looking at the academic achievement of home educated children in the United States, it is useful to consider the work of Raymond and Dorothy Moore (1975) (see Chapter 2). When the Moores commenced their research they were not fully committed to home education. However, they found significant disadvantages in early schooling, ranging from juvenile delinquency and behavioural problems to near-sightedness. There was a definite and measurable correlation between the age formal schooling began and numerous subsequent difficulties. They argued that the emotional bonds being developed between the child and her parents were cut short when formal schooling began, and that this had tragic and irreversible consequences.

The Moores cited many studies which showed that children who were removed from home during the day to the institutional setting of school remained socially and emotionally immature. They compared their findings with the research on children from societies where early formal education in school is all but unknown. Such children were found to be more socially adept and emotionally stable than western children who had attended kindergartens and nurseries from an early age. Their quantifiable research echoes much of what John Bowlby found in his work on maternal deprivation in the UK (Bowlby, 1979) and indicates one reason why some home educating parents are strongly opposed to sending their children off to nursery or school when they are very young.

Possibly the largest single study of educational attainment in home education was conducted in 1998. Data were collected on the academic achievements, home backgrounds and other information of over 20,000 home educated children in the United States and sent to an independent expert, Lawrence Rudner, for analysis. Although the Home School Legal Defence Association financed this study, those carrying it out and collating the results were not home educators, nor were they involved in home education. Rudner's work was subsequently published in a peer reviewed journal.

Several features marked this study out from previous research projects on home education in the US. First, the study was objective. Second, the parents agreed to be included in the survey before they knew what their children's test results were, so there was no bias in favour of high scores, a factor which had skewed previous studies in favour of home education. Third, the survey used the same test on all the children: the Iowa Test of Basic Skills (Rudner, 1999).

The findings were encouraging to home educators. Home educated children did better than those at school in every subject and every age group. As in the UK, children at private schools in the US generally do better than those in maintained schools – but the home-schooled children outperformed both. Most surprising was the finding that the longer children were home educated, the better their academic achievement. The highest achievers were those who had never been to school at all.

Factors in the lives of these children were sought to account for their academic success. Their parents were found to be educated to a higher level than average. In a quarter of the families one or both parents were qualified teachers. The percentage of parents who were married was higher than the national average, perhaps connected with the fact that many were devoutly religious, primarily evangelical Christians. The mothers tended to stay at home or work only part-time. The picture was of conventional families in which the father goes out to work and the mother stays at home with the children and the whole family worship in church on Sundays. Only 6 per cent of the families studied were from ethnic minority communities, as compared with around 30 per cent nationally.

A picture emerges of stable and traditional white families who are dissatisfied with the schools system because it does not educate children effectively and transmits poor ethical values to children. The parents in these families are sure they can do better themselves – and the findings confirm this to be the case.

There has been some criticism of these data, mainly because most of the home educated children took the tests on a voluntary basis. All children and young people take such tests in the public (maintained) schools in the US, with the consequence that in one case a whole population is being tested and in the other only a self-selected group. So bias cannot be ruled out. Added to this is the suspicion that anybody investigating home education is unlikely to be entirely impartial.

A more objective measure of the academic ability of home educated young people is a test taken by many teenagers, both schooled and home educated. Americans wishing to gain admission to colleges and universities sit either the SAT or ACT test. In the last few years students taking these tests have been specifically asked whether or not they have been home educated. These tests show home educated students to be ahead of those who attended school, but by a narrower margin than as reported by other researchers (Des Moine Register, 2004). On the ACT college entrance test, for instance, it is possible to score from one to 36. Schooled students average about 21, while those who have been home educated come in at almost 23.

The individual components are particularly revealing. In reading, the home educated are greatly ahead of average. They are roughly level in science and slightly behind in mathematics.

These data from colleges reveal another interesting statistic. The proportion of home educated students who take the SAT and ACT tests for college entrance is lower than expected, given the number of home educated children in the US, so home educated children appear to be less likely than those who have attended school to apply for a place at college or university. Home education organisations in America challenge this assertion, suggesting that some students seek to conceal the fact that they are home educated when they apply to college. Possibly they fear prejudice, although in reality, some universities give preference to such students.

The tests taken by those wishing to go to college or university are also self-selected in that only those who wish to study at college take them. The overall analysis of students who take the SAT or ACT tests suggests that fewer home educated young people apply to college or university but that those who do so are more academically accomplished in some areas than those who attended school. Although interesting, this is not the dramatic endorsement of the educational advantages offered by home education that some would claim.

The picture in American home education is so different from the British scene, both in family structure and motivation, that it is doubtful that the broad conclusions of American research in this field can be applied uncritically to home education in Britain.

There is some anecdotal evidence that typical British home educators are unlikely to match the profile of the American families and more likely to be single mothers. If she has to bear sole responsibility for running the home, as well as for educating a child, a mother will have pressing calls upon her time and energies. It may be easier when there are two people undertaking the child's education and having a man living in the household might have implications for certain aspects of education. So it is difficult to know how much of the academic success of the children in American studies is due to their having been home educated, and how much is a result of a family structure and socio-economic background which is known to support children's academic achievement whatever their educational setting.

In the western countries studied, education *per se* seems not to be the main reason for parents to keep their children from school. Family relationships appear to be seen as at least as important as education. According to Thomas and Pattinson, who looked at home educating families in the UK and Australia:

> Many parents point out that their reasons for home educating have as much to do with social and personal development as with academic progress... This aspect of home education may turn out to be very beneficial. (Thomas and Pattison, 2007)

Thomas's research differs from most of the other work discussed here, which focus upon the family circumstances, motives or academic achievement of home educated children and their families. He explored the actual methods used by home educators (Thomas, 1994). This was based upon a study of 23 home educating families, who had between them 40 children aged between five and thirteen.

Thomas found that although many of the families in his study had started off aiming for a conventional teaching regimen, almost all dropped this after they had been home educating for a while. Formal teaching was transmuted into developing more casual, informal learning in an everyday context. The large amount of one-to-one contact the children in this study had with an attentive adult enabled them to pick up a great deal of knowledge in an apparently random and haphazard fashion. Thomas concluded that the actual style of education did not much matter. The main factor in the education which he observed was the amount of one-to-one contact the children had with adults.

In the late 1980s Julie Webb conducted research in England and spent time getting close to home educating families. She came to broadly similar conclusions to Thomas: learning at home was effective (Webb, 1990). She found that learning was not constrained by lack of money or equipment. Even subjects like physics, chemistry and biology, the effective home teaching of which are viewed with scepticism by secondary school science teachers, she found to be tackled successfully up to GCSE level by all the parents who wished to do so. She was struck by the resourcefulness of home educators, who always seemed to find a way of solving whatever problems arose. Scientific experiments were conducted at the kitchen sink using improvised materials, augmented where necessary by chemistry sets and the use of laboratories at local schools (Webb, 1990).

Strengths of their own: Home Schoolers across America (Ray, 1997) documented research in the US into the educational attainment of home educated children. Brian Ray's study of over 5000 home educated children found that home educated children outperformed those in public schools in every area. Interestingly, Ray found, as did Rudner, that the longer a child was home educated, the greater the academic advantage.

Ray also found that home education, as well as being effective, was also cheap. Parents were typically spending less than a tenth as much as education departments on their child's education yet getting far better results. Strict regulation of home education did not affect the children's educational attainment. Whether or not the state laws insisted on dictating a curriculum and required parents to hold a teaching certificate was irrelevant to outcomes (Ray, 1997). This finding might have bearing on the current debate in England about whether new laws are needed to regulate home education.

Ofsted's research in 2010 is the most recent attempt to gather a large amount of data about home educating families. In 2009, a questionnaire was distributed to home educators known to fifteen local authorities. Immediately, some parents and home education organisations objected. Appeals were made on Internet lists for home educators to boycott the research, although the questionnaire was innocuous. Parents were asked, for instance, why they had de-registered their child from school, and whether the child had special educational needs. But certain questions caused outrage: 'What sort of curriculum does your child follow?' and the next: 'On average how many hours a day does your child study? 1 2 3 4 5 6'

The Internet lists overflowed with indignation. Strong objections were made to the series of questions about the sort of activities the children took part in, such as ballet, martial arts, football, pottery, on the grounds that Ofsted did not ask parents of school educated children such intrusive questions.

Despite this hostility, Ofsted held face-to-face talks with two hundred and fifty parents and children and received over three hundred responses to their questionnaires. Visits were made to fourteen local authorities and the views of local authority officers were gathered.

A third of the parents had removed their children from school because they were bullied. A quarter of the children had special educational needs. These figures resonate with previous research. Most parents had de-registered their children from school rather than never sending them to school. Many of the parents wanted more access to services – the taking of examinations without charge was shown to be a major issue. For the local authorities, the main problem was their inability to find out how many home educated children were in their area and they were consequently unanimous in calling for compulsory registration.

The ill-feeling that followed Ofsted's attempt to discover something about home education demonstrated why solid information is so hard to come by. Home educating parents can be touchy. In February 2010, the DCSF, now the Department for Education, announced that it intended to commission a study to investigate the feasibility of embarking on a longitudinal project to investigate the provision of teaching and learning for, and the attainment of, home-educated children. Already there are rumblings of suspicion and discontent.

5

The legal situation

Home education has never been illegal in Britain. Even with the advent of universal schooling in Britain in 1870, a loophole was retained for home education for those who wished to take up the option. Introducing the Elementary Education Act to the Commons on February 17th 1870, W.E. Forster said:

> We give power to the school boards to frame bye-laws for compulsory atten-
> dance of all children within their district from five to twelve. They must see
> that no parent is under a penalty for not sending his child to school if he can
> show reasonable excuse; reasonable excuse being education elsewhere, or
> sickness... (Forster, 1870)

Just as in the later 1944 Education Act with its 'by regular attendance at school or otherwise', so Forster's act contained a get out clause, 'education elsewhere'.

For the best part of a century after the establishment of Universal Schooling, some parents, mainly the wealthier ones, chose not to send their children to school. They were never in danger of breaking the law. Today, the situation is more complicated than it was even a few years ago. The law relating to home education is covered by a complex and confusing mix of statute law and precedent or case law.

Case law differs from statute law. Laws passed by Parliament are known as statute law. When cases are heard in court, magistrates and judges have to interpret these laws and decide how they apply in a real life situation. These decisions are known as precedent and they can be as binding as statute law on those conducting future court cases. Almost all the law relating to home education is case law rather than statute. An attempt was made in the wake of the Badman Report to revise the law and bring every aspect of home education into one clear and un-ambiguous piece of legislation but this failed. The relevant schedule in the Bill did not reach the Statute Book before the 2010 election brought a change of government.

The basic law relating to home education is to be found in Section 7 of the 1996 Education Act which states that:

> The parent of every child of compulsory school age shall cause him to re-ceive efficient full-time education suitable –
>
> (a) to his age, ability and aptitude, and
>
> (b) to any special educational needs he may have, either by regular atten-dance at school or otherwise. (Education Act, 1996)

The 1996 Act failed to define what is meant by 'efficient', 'full-time' or 'suitable'. In order to see what these terms might mean, we are obliged to delve into old cases, some of which date back almost a century.

An 'efficient' education was described by Lord Alverstone in his judge-ment in *Bevan v Shears* 1911, one of the key cases for home educators. He said:

> In the absence of anything in the bye-laws providing that a child of a given age shall receive instruction in given subjects, in my view it cannot be said that there is a standard of education by which the child must be taught. The court has to decide whether in their opinion the child is being taught effi-ciently so far as that particular child is concerned. (Alverstone, 1911)

Lord Alverstone went on to rule that in the case of a child being taught out of school, a court could decide for themselves, on evidence pro-vided, whether the education was in fact efficient. They could do this without any reference to the standard or type of education being pro-vided by schools. This precedent is still binding today and means that if a local authority prosecutes a parent for not following the terms of a School Attendance Order, the court can make up their own mind about whether the child is actually receiving an education which is 'efficient', regardless of what a school might be teaching a child of that age. There are however moves afoot to define precisely what is meant by 'suitable' or 'efficient' education. If they wish to formulate a definition, any govern-ment of the day can use a Statutory Instrument to make this legally binding upon local authorities and parents. This was one of the aims of the new legislation which the Labour Government attempted to intro-duce. A clear definition of an 'efficient education' would probably make life considerably easier for local authority officers charged with the inspection of home educating families.

The definition of an 'efficient' education was expanded in another case, that of *R v Secretary of State for Education and Science, ex parte Talmud Torah Machzeikei Hadass School Trust*, 1985. Mr. Justice Woolf gave it as his opinion that an 'efficient' education was one that 'achieves what it sets out to achieve.' In the course of the same judgement, he described a 'suitable' education as one which, 'primarily equips a child for life within the community of which he is a member, rather than the way of life in the country as a whole' (Woolf, 1985).

It is the parent who has responsibility for seeing that the child receives an education, not the state or the local authority. Also part of this hodgepodge of old laws and precedent which covers home education is the area of special educational needs, first mentioned in the Education Act 1981. Section 36 of the 1944 Education Act was amended, so that it now talked of the parents' duty to provide an efficient, full-time educa-tion suitable to the child's 'age, ability and aptitude and to any special educational needs which he might have, either by regular attendance at school or otherwise'.

It seems clear that, when it comes to deregistering and teaching a child at home, a child with special needs is in the same position as one without. Well, yes and no. Because the Education (Pupil Registration) (England) Regulations 2006, which cover the deregistration of children from school to be home educated, contain the following provision: Regulation 8 (1)(d) states that a child's name is to be removed from a school's register if

> he has ceased to attend the school and the proprietor has received written notification from the parent that the pupil is receiving education otherwise than at school.

Thus, writing a letter to the school asking them to remove the child from the register is normally all that is required. However, Regulation 8 (2) goes on to say that if the child is attending a Special School, the permission of the local authority is needed before he can be removed from the roll. In practice permission is seldom withheld but the fact that it can be more difficult to de-register a child with special educational needs or disabilities and teach her at home has been thought by some to be a contravention of the various laws which prevent discrimination against children who have a disability.

The legal situation in respect of home education is further complicated by the Children Act 2004 and the local authority's duty to see that all the children in its area are safe, well and have access to the five outcomes of the *Every Child Matters* agenda. These outcomes, which are legally underpinned by the Children Act, are: to be healthy, to stay safe, to enjoy and achieve, to make a positive contribution and to achieve economic wellbeing.

The passage of this act has made the situation around home education immeasurably more complicated for all concerned. Local authorities are obliged by law to check that children not at school are receiving a full time education suitable to their age and ability, and they are now charged also with ensuring that they are being given access to the five outcomes of the ECM agenda. It is not easy to ascertain all this in the course of a one hour visit each year. And if the family refuse to allow an officer from the local authority even to visit, it becomes impossible.

Making the local authority responsible for seeing that all the children in their area are being given access to the five outcomes can bring them into conflict with some home educators. There were similar problems with an amendment to the Education Act 1996, Section 436A, which placed a duty upon local authorities to identify children missing from education. Section 437 specified that home educated children receiving a suitable education are not to be regarded as being missing from education. So local authorities must seek out children who are not receiving a suitable education. But can local authority officers tell whether a home educated child is receiving a suitable education? The local authority will try to do this by going and seeing the children and talking to their parents. However the parents often take the view that it should be assumed that they are providing their children with a suitable education unless there is any evidence to the contrary. Local authorities find some home educating parents difficult to deal with and parents feel that local authorities have all the powers they need to tackle parents whom they decide are not providing their children with a suitable education.

What can a local authority do if they suspect that a child is not being educated? The first step is to write to the parents and ask them for evidence that an education is being given to the child. If this does not satisfy them, they can serve a notice on the parents, giving them fifteen days either to satisfy the authority that their child is receiving suitable full-time education or to register her at a school. If neither of these things are done, a School Attendance Order can be issued. This names a school where the child must be registered as a pupil. If the parents ignore this, the way is open for the local authority to bring a prosecution.

The issuing of School Attendance Orders and prosecutions for disobeying them are rare. Since there is no clear definition of what constitutes a proper education, a parent might well persuade a magistrate that she is providing a suitable education, whatever provision she makes, in which case the prosecution will fail. Local authorities know this and, unless they are absolutely sure of success, tend to avoid taking the matter to court (CSF select committee, 2009), as this entails having legal representation themselves and preparing a great deal of paperwork. Ofsted's survey of local authorities in 2009 discovered that of fifteen local authorities, ten had not issued any School Attendance Orders in connection with home education in the preceding year and five had each issued one (Ofsted, 2010).

A local authority can also try and obtain an Education Supervision Order. This means that parents and child must cooperate with social workers and so on and make sure that the child attends school regularly. These too are used sparingly.

It has been clear for some years that this confusing collection of statute law and precedent satisfies neither parents nor local authority officers. But the more the law is tinkered with, the more that local authorities and home educating parents have came into conflict over their differing interpretations of the legal situation.

Following the York Consulting study (see Chapter 5), the Department for Children, Schools and Families issued *Guidelines for Local Authorities*

(DCSF, 2007). These set out what was thought to be the legal position for local authorities when monitoring home education. These guidelines were greeted with enthusiasm by parents but irritation by most local authority officers. Local authorities had been hoping for increased powers: instead, they found their ability to act curtailed by new and official government advice. Section 2.5, for example, says:

> Parents are not required to register or seek approval from the local authority to educate their children at home. Parents who choose to educate their children at home must be prepared to assume full financial responsibility, including bearing the cost of any public examinations. However, local authorities are encouraged to provide support where resources permit – see section 5. (DCSF, 2007)

In other words, parents still did not need to notify their local authority of their intention to teach a child at home, but at the same time the authority should be ready with support if necessary. The sentence in the guidelines which caused most problems for local authorities was a line in section 2.7: 'Local authorities have no statutory duties in relation to monitoring the quality of home education on a routine basis' (DCSF, 2007).

Local authority officers attempting to check on home educated children found the above line quoted to them by parents who refused them access to their homes or sight of their children. Sections from the guidelines were circulated on Internet sites run by home educators, and local authorities found their hands tied unless they had evidence of safeguarding concerns or a strong indication that a suitable education was not being provided for a child. The following year a tragedy occurred which persuaded the then Secretary of State for Education, Ed Balls, that the situation regarding home education needed to be urgently reviewed.

In December 2007 a seven year old girl called Khyra Ishaq was withdrawn from school in Birmingham to be educated at home. The school were uneasy about this and staff visited the child's home. Over the next few months, efforts were made to find out more about the situation, but the mother, Angela Gordon, was well informed about her legal rights. After one visit, she made an accusation of racism and harassment in order to prevent further interference. In May 2008, Khyra Ishaq died of complications caused by malnutrition.

As the details of the Khyra Ishaq case gradually emerged, what had long been apparent to local authorities became increasingly clear to those at the DCSF; that the situation regarding the monitoring and supervision of elective home education in England was profoundly unsatisfactory. In January 2009, Ed Balls asked Graham Badman, formerly Managing Director of the Children, Families and Education Directorate for Kent County Council, to review the arrangements for home education in England. In particular, he was to see whether there were any barriers to local authorities and other public agencies in carrying out their safeguarding responsibilities in regard to home educated children. The terms of reference were to look at:

- The barriers to local authorities and other public agencies in carrying out their responsibilities for safeguarding home educated children and advise on improvements to ensure that the five Every Child Matters outcomes are being met for home educated children

- The extent to which claims of home education could be used as a 'cover' for child abuse such as neglect, forced marriage, sexual exploitation or domestic servitude and advise on measures to prevent this

- Whether local authorities are providing the right type, level and balance of support to home educating families to ensure they are undertaking their duties to provide a suitable full-time education to their children

- Whether any changes to the current regime for monitoring the standard of home education are needed to support the work of parents, local authorities and other partners in ensuring all children achieve the Every Child Matters outcomes. (Badman, 2009)

In order to investigate these four points, Badman solicited views from parents, children, local authorities and anybody else who wished to offer an opinion. Among those who gave their views were the Association of Directors of Children's Services, the Foreign and Commonwealth Office Forced Marriage Unit, the NSPCC and many other organisations.

From the start Badman was willing to talk to anybody involved in any way with home education. He received submissions from home educators themselves, as well as from support groups like Education Otherwise and HEAS. In addition to taking written submissions he met parents and professionals in face to face interviews and had telephone conversations with those who could not meet him in person. Despite the later bitter criticism which his report attracted, he appeared to approach the task with an open mind.

As had been expected, most parents who responded to the review wished to be left alone, while the majority of professionals wanted greater involvement of local authorities and other agencies in the lives of home educating families. Local authorities seemed to be unanimous in their demands for increased powers to monitor children being educated at home. Without exception, they claimed that existing statute and case law did not meet the case. They believed that unless all children being educated at home could be registered and their whereabouts known, some would inevitably slip through the net and be lost to sight. Some of these hidden children could come to harm.

In June 2009, Badman published his report, which contained twenty eight recommendations. Three of these recommendations are likely to form the basis for any future legislation on home education in Britain. Although the part of the Children, Schools and Families Bill 2009 which was based on these recommendations failed to become law due to the calling of the general election in May 2010, the matter is far from resolved and, at the time of writing in late 2010, demands are increasingly being made to consider once again the introduction of a new law on home educating. Most of Badman's recommendations were unexceptionable, such as Recommendation 9, which urges:

> That all local authority officers and others engaged in the monitoring and support of elective home education must be suitably trained. This training must include awareness of safeguarding issues and a full understanding of the essential difference, variation and diversity in home education practice, as compared to schools. Wherever possible and appropriate, representatives of the home educating community should be involved in the development and/or provision of such training. (Badman Report, 2009)

Other recommendations were more controversial. The main planks of the new system which Badman was suggesting were contained in recommendations 1, 2 and 7. The proposals caused huge disquiet among home educators and are discussed below.

Recommendation 1

- That the DCSF establishes a compulsory national registration scheme, locally administered, for all children of statutory school age, who are, or become, electively home educated.

- This scheme should be common to all local authorities.

- Registration should be renewed annually.

- Those who are registering for the first time should be visited by the appropriate local authority officer within one moth of registration

- Local authorities should ensure that all home educated children and young people already known to them are registered on the new scheme within one month of its inception and visited over the following twelve months, following the commencement of any new legislation.

- Provision should be made to allow registration at a local school, children's centre or other public building as determined by the local authority.

- When parents are thinking of deregistering their child/children from school to home educate, schools should retain such pupils on roll for a period of 20 school days so that should there be a change in circumstances, the child could be readmitted to the school. This period was also allow for the resolution of such difficulties that may have prompted the decision to remove the child from school.

- National guidance should be issued on the requirements of registration and be made available online and at appropriate public buildings. Such guidance must include a clear statement of the statutory basis of elective home education and the rights and responsibilities of parents.

- At the time of registration parents/carers/guardians must provide a clear statement of their educational approach, intent and desired/planned outcomes for the child over the next twelve months.

Recommendation 2 asked the DCSF to review the definition of an 'efficient' and 'suitable' education. Recommendation 7 sent shockwaves through the home educating community. The proposal was:

That designated local authority officers should:

- have the right of access to the home

- have the right to speak with each child alone if deemed appropriate or if a child is particularly vulnerable or had particular communication needs, in the company of a trusted person who is not the home educator or the parent/carer.

The rationale was that if a child were frightened of his parents, he might be more likely to open up to sympathetic adults if the parents were not in the same room. However, the impression was conveyed that home educated children were more likely to need this type of interview than those at school.

Annual renewal of registration and the requirement for a statement of desired outcomes over the next twelve months was another idea which made parents uneasy. Some felt that this provided for a system of licensing for home educators.

When the Badman report was published, the Secretary of State for Education announced that he accepted the findings and recommendations in full. Subsequently a Commons select committee decided to hold a brief investigation into the conduct of the review. They invited written submissions and in October 2009 summoned various witnesses to give evidence. Their report, which was published in December 2009, accepted most of the recommendations made in the Badman report. The few changes suggested by the select committee did not satisfy either parents or the DCSF and some seemed to make little sense. On the subject of registration, for example, the select committee wanted it to be voluntary to begin with. They went on to say:

> The success of a system of voluntary registration (combined with improved information sharing) should be reviewed after two years. If it is found not to have met expectations – in terms of assisting local authorities in identifying and working with the families of children who are being home educated and those of children not otherwise at school – we believe that a system if compulsory registration would need to be introduced. (CSF select committee, 2009)

In other words, the system would be voluntary for two years and then if all home educating parents did not sign up voluntarily then they would be made to do so.

The Queen's speech at the opening of parliament in November 2009 included mention of a new Bill, The Children, Schools and families Bill, which included regulations for the registration and monitoring of elective home education. The actual content was as expected.

Several of the provisions caused anger and dismay among some home educators. For instance, the process of registration was to include the provision by a parent of ' a statement giving prescribed information about the child's prospective education'. What was this 'prescribed information'? Did this mean that home educating parents would be legally required to work to a curriculum? Nobody knew. The wording of the regulations was so vague as to be almost meaningless. Some of the specific requirements were hedged in with the proviso that these should be carried out – 'as far as is reasonably practicable'. The explanation for all this emerged gradually over the following days. The Bill was really in the nature of an enabling act. It would set up a framework in law and the details would then be filled in by civil servants at a later date. These details could themselves be altered as and when any subsequent government saw fit.

This is not an unusual procedure. The amendments are known as Statutory Instruments and can be enacted without returning to parliament for further legislation. What made home educators suspicious was that the regulations were so vague that they left open the possibility of the most sweeping future powers and ferocious restrictions on home education. Nobody could tell from reading the draft regulations, what would actually happen.

Significantly, however, Schedule 1 of the bill made provision for the registration of all home educated children. The responsibility for this was to rest with local authorities. It had been feared that it would become a criminal offence for parents to fail to register their child for home education or to move to another district without notifying their new local authority of their intention to teach their child at home, but this did not prove to be the case.

Another recommendation in the Badman report was that local authority officers monitoring home education should have a right of entry to the homes of children being taught at home. In the regulations as finally published, this had been watered down into a duty upon the local authority for 'visiting, at least once in the registration period, the place (or at least one of the places) where education is provided to the child' (CSF Bill, 2009), such as a library instead of the family home. Even this was qualified by being described as one of those 'arrangements made with a view' to doing certain things. It was by no means certain that even this proposal would actually be mandatory for local authorities.

Interviewing children alone, an idea which caused alarm among home educating parents, was also dropped. In the Bill it was recommended that this should only happen if both parent and child agree. Even the police cannot demand access to people's homes and speak to their children alone unless they have a strong suspicion that a crime has been committed.

Parents remained apprehensive about these recommended powers. For instance, the registration itself was contingent upon the co-operation of the parents with such matters as providing a statement of their educational approach. While the local authority would not be given the power to enter homes, it was made clear that refusal to allow access to the child would be grounds for the revocation of registration. This would pave the way for the automatic issue of a School Attendance Order.

The Bill set out other duties for the local authority, but it is enough for now to know that local authorities would have had a duty to discover home educated children and register them. They would also be legally responsible for monitoring home education. As noted, successful prosecutions for breaching School Attendance Orders are rare at the moment because it is hard to establish whether or not a child is receiving a suitable education. This difficulty would have vanished once the Bill came into force. A child would be assumed to be receiving a suitable education if either at school or registered as a home educated child with the local authority. If the local authority withdrew or refused the registration, he would not be receiving a suitable education and must be sent to school. Nobody knows what the courts would have made of this.

I have outlined those provisions dealing with home education in the CSF Bill because even though they did not become law, many in both the Department for Education and local authorities feel that it is only a matter of time before new legislation does alter the position for home education in Britain. Any new law would probably be very similar to Schedule 1 of the CSF Bill. In Chapter 7 I propose a new regulatory system for home education in the United Kingdom which is based upon the provisions discussed above.

Badman's review applied only to England and Schedule 1 of the CSF Bill would have been limited to England, although there were plans to extend its provisions to Wales. In Northern Ireland, the legal position is much the same as it is for England and Wales. In Scotland the situation is, and looks likely to remain, somewhat different.

In Scotland, the right to home educate is covered by two acts. Section 14 of the Standards in Scotland's Schools Act 2000 says that Scottish Ministers may issue guidance according to the circumstances in which parents may educate their children at home. This guidance supplements the Education (Scotland) Act 1980, which itself states that it is the duty of parents to provide efficient education for their children either by regular attendance at school or otherwise. So far, so like the law in England – but there is one important difference.

If a child in Scotland has never attended a state funded school, or has finished primary school and not yet started secondary school or been withdrawn from an independent school, there is no requirement for the parents to seek permission or indeed notify anybody of their intention to home educate. If they wish to withdraw a child from a state funded school, parents must obtain permission to do so and this permission will be granted or withheld depending upon the educational provision which the parents intend to make for their child. If the new act had been passed and seen to be working efficiently, both Scotland and Northern Ireland might well have introduced legislation of their own modelled upon it. The British arrangements for home educators remain among the most relaxed to be found anywhere. In most other countries home education is both possible and accepted, or at least tolerated, to varying degrees. In very few is it banned entirely.

The US has, as we have seen, far the greatest number of home educated children. Different laws and regulations apply to each state. None ban it entirely, although there are periodic attempts to do so, most recently in California. The laws in Colorado are fairly typical (Colorado Department of Education, 1963). All parents can teach their own children at their own expense. It is not necessary to be a qualified teacher, a restriction applied in some states. Colorado has a rough definition of what constitutes full-time education. Parents are required to teach their children for no fewer than 172 days a year and each teaching day must include four hours actual work with the child. A sparse and basic curriculum is defined by state law. Subjects covered should include reading, writing, mathematics, history, science, literature, civics and the United

States constitution. Records must be kept of attendance, tests taken and immunisation.

Other states vary greatly in their requirements. Some like Texas and Alaska have limited regulation and do not define what constitutes a full-time education. The strictest states, such as New York and North Dakota, impose strong and some would say prohibitive rules on home education. Parents must have a teaching certificate, accept home visits, register with the state, use an approved curriculum and sometimes allow mandatory testing of children in public schools so their progress can be assessed.

These widely differing rules are of interest because, as we have seen, stricter regulations seem to have no effect upon the academic achievement of the children. Possibly since so many home educating American parents are traditional families who teach their children for educational purposes, the general academic level is bound to be high, whatever the laws.

The law relating to French home education is interesting. When changed almost two decades ago, there were fears that this was the beginning of the end for home education in the country. Some British parents feared that it was part of a wider trend in the countries of the EU which could eventually see the total abolition of home education. In 1998, a law was passed in France which introduced compulsory registration for home educators. The following year, another law was passed which set out what children educated at home should be studying. It also declared that home educated children should be at roughly the same academic standard by the age of sixteen as those taught at school. The subjects studied had to include the French language, knowledge of French literature, history and geography, mathematics, science and technology, sport and art (Taylor and Petrie, 2000).

Despite these restrictions, there is no sign of the French home education scene dwindling away. The idea that this was an attack on home education was not borne out by subsequent events. If anything, home education in France seems now to be more robust and better organised than before.

Every time a European country attempts to regulate the practice of home education, some parents in Britain express the fear that this will mark the beginning of the end for home education in Europe, which will inevitably involve the UK. What they fear is that other countries are looking to Germany and that the German example might become widespread throughout Europe. Germany is the ultimate nightmare for home educators.

The law in Germany requires all children to attend school. This law dates from the Nazi era and has never been repealed. Parents in Germany who have withdrawn their children from schools to teach them at home have been fined, sent to prison and have even had their children removed and taken into care. Some recent cases have involved devout Christians who wished to raise their children according to their own values and not those of the state.

One such case was taken to the Federal Constitutional Court of Germany, which upheld the ban on home education. In 2003 this case reached the European Court of Human Rights. The implications of the judgement made there has troubled home educators in Britain. The parent who brought the case argued that Germany's ban on home education contravened the Charter of Fundamental Rights of the European Union, which provides that a state shall respect parents' rights to ensure that their child's education will be in conformity with their own religious and philosophical beliefs.

In September 2006, The European Court gave its ruling. In its opinion the plaintiff in the case was not the parent but the children. They ruled that children were unable to foresee the consequences of their parents' decision to home educate, due to their young age. They further stated that schools were part of society and that the rights of parents did not extend so far as for them to be able to deprive children of their place in society (*Brussels Journal*, 2006).

This was a blow for families in Germany. It also made home educating parents elsewhere in Europe fear that there was nothing to stop Britain or any country in Europe from banning home education entirely.

In January 2010, a judge in Memphis, USA, granted political asylum to a family of German home educators who had fled their country. The judge ruled that they belonged to a persecuted minority and that Germany was disregarding human rights by its insistence on children attending school (*New York Times*, 2010).

The law in Holland is almost as strict as in Germany. It is just about possible for a parents to argue that the strength of their philosophical or religious beliefs does not permit them to allow their children to attend school. But this is difficult, so fewer than a hundred children are kept out of school. Moreover, even this option is not open once a child has been registered at a school. It is presumed that the act of registering a child at school means that parents accept the idea of schooling.

Sweden too has recently adopted a hard line on home education. There are few home educators in the country, but there may soon be none at all. In June 2010 the Swedish parliament approved a law which would ban home education being undertaken for religious or philosophical reasons. The only time when it might be permitted would be in 'extraordinary circumstances'. It is not yet clear what these circumstances might be, but they probably include bullying with which the school is unable to deal. This same law also imposed a state curriculum upon all schools, including the so-called free schools. The intention is that every child in the country will be receiving a standard, government approved education. Again, British parents view these developments with alarm lest they are part of a new trend.

Because of the sheer size of the country and the relative sparsity of the population, home education in Australia has always been tolerated. One state of Australia in particular has attracted the attention of British parents for its approach to home education. The so-called 'Tasmanian Model' is described in Chapter 7. Briefly, home educators themselves run the monitoring and registration system in Tasmania and it all seems to work well.

The experience of New Zealand is also instructive. At one time, the authorities insisted on annual visits to home educating families to check that their children were well and being properly educated. The requirement has been dropped because almost all the monitoring visits were found to be a waste of time. It was decided instead to focus time and energy upon families who actually needed help, rather than the scattergun approach of trying to see everybody regularly (CSF select committee, 2009).

One of the problems with seeing thousands of families regularly and trying to spot problems is that this will generate false positives: you identify those who look as though they have difficulties but actually do not. Time is thus wasted upon cases which do not need help. The larger the group one looks at, the more of these false positives are liable to crop up. So there is good reason to try and keep the target group as small as possible.

Home educators in Britain who are facing, as they see it, new restrictions upon their 'right' to home educate are raising a legal point in reaction to the failed attempt by German home educators to appeal to the provisions of the European Convention on Human Rights. They claim that the United Nations Convention on the Rights of the Child (UNCRC) would establish their rights to educate their children as they see fit, but this is unlikely. The UNCRC sets out quite a prescriptive basis for education, which is regarded as an entitlement of the child, not a right of the parent. Article 29 states:

State Parties agree that the education of the child shall be directed to:

(a) The development of the child's personality, talents and mental and physical abilities to their fullest potential;

(b) The development of respect for human rights and fundamental freedoms, and for the freedoms enshrined in the Charter of the United Nations;

(c) The development of respect for the child's parents, his or her own cultural identity, language and values, for the national values of the country in which the child is living, the country from which he or she may originate, and for civilisations different from his or her own;

(d) The preparation of the child for responsible life in a free society, in the spirit of understanding, peace, tolerance, equality of sexes, and friendship of all peoples, ethnic, national and religious groups and persons of indigenous origin;

(e) The development of respect for the natural environment. (United Nations, 1989)

Any parents thinking of appealing to the United Nations about some supposed infringement of their 'rights' would do well to ensure that the education which they were providing for their child actually fulfils all the stiff criteria contained in the UNCRC.

6

Home education – for and against

The areas of controversy associated with home education include safeguarding concerns on the part of local authorities, worries about socialisation and the difficulties associated with home educated children taking examinations. Local authorities are not the only ones who have reservations about the benefits of home education as it is practiced in the UK. Other bodies have opinions on the matter and many people are puzzled and a little dubious about home education. Home educating parents have their own views on these matters and they feel that their lifestyle is seriously misunderstood.

We have looked briefly at a few of the objections raised about elective home education and how these are countered by home educators. Many of these questions are not about education as such, but relate rather to the overall lifestyle of home educating families. In this chapter I look in depth at four areas where the views of home educators differ from most other people, both lay and professional. These are socialisation, safeguarding, examinations and religion and ethnicity.

Socialisation
Peer pressure
This is the question all home educators expect to be asked, sooner rather than later: 'What about socialisation?' Or it may be presented in other forms, 'Doesn't your son get lonely?' or 'Do you think she misses her friends at school?' The suggestion is that there is something pretty weird about a child spending much time with her parents and that she will

become a lonely, introverted creature, unable to relate appropriately to others of the same age. Home educated children will, it is hinted, become isolated and unable to interact normally with other children because of their supposed lack of regular contact with their peer group.

No chance to hang around with friends in the playground, talk about music and popular culture. She is bound to be out of touch. How will she be when she is older? A childhood like this could scar her for life. She may never recover, never be able to form normal relationships with others as a direct result of her strange and atypical upbringing.

This is no exaggeration – parents and professionals do say such things about home educated children, although not always to the parents' faces. But how do most parents of school children really view socialisation? Parents who have children at school seldom talk about 'socialisation' – they talk about 'peer pressure' and most regard it in a negative light.

Outside the industrialised West, culture and moral values are transmitted vertically, from adults to children. This used to be the case in Britain and the rest of the western world, but in the last sixty years or so it has changed radically. Children now learn their culture horizontally, from other children (Rutter and Smith, 1995). Many believe this to be a bad thing.

Most children no longer look to the generation above them to learn how to behave: instead they turn to each other. They tell each other what clothes to wear, how to speak, what music to listen to, whether to engage in sexual activity and if so what sort, what drugs to take, how much alcohol to drink, so that practically every aspect of the average child's life is heavily influenced by the views of his fellow pupils at school.

Peer pressure is, moreover, an historical aberration. For most of recorded history, children and young people looked to their parents and other adults as mentors who would teach them how to behave and show them the best way of doing things. Clearly, the best person to demonstrate responsible alcohol use is more likely to be a grown man or woman than another teenager. In the same way, an adult is more likely to be able to teach the child how to live normally and find his place in society (Neufeld and Gabe, 2004). Adults in general and parents in particular have abdicated their responsibilities in this matter, responsibilities which home educators are eager to reclaim.

Home educating parents reject the whole argument about 'socialisation'. and most parents of school-going children will concede that the home educators may have a point. Rarely does one hear a mother saying, ' I'm so pleased with the way John has started speaking, now that he is at secondary school' or 'Mary has picked up some wonderful habits from her friends at school'.

Social skills

Home educated children are not kept closeted away from their contemporaries and they routinely associate with other young people. In addition to groups run for home educating parents and their children by organisations such as Education Otherwise, there are all the usual children's out of school activities. Brownies and cubs, Woodcraft Folk, Duke of Edinburgh Award, Sunday schools, complementary places of worship, dance classes – the list is endless. Any child who is not attending school can see as much or as little of other children as she wishes (Farris, 1997).

The socialisation of children educated out of school often tends to be more natural and extensive than for those who learn in the classroom (Rudner, 1999; Shyers, 1992). At school, children are kept to one peer group, which varies in age by no more than twelve months. Schoolchildren soon learn that friendships with others who are a little older or younger can bring mockery or disapproval from their peers. The unspoken rule is, 'Stick to your own age group'. This is a peculiar idea and one which will not be encountered by the child again, certainly not in adult life.

There is also the artificial respect and formality for the adults at the school, exemplified by the use of words such as 'Sir' and 'Miss', which creates a strange and somewhat anachronistic atmosphere in which the child becomes immersed.

However, the average home educated child mixes regularly with people of all ages. Babies, toddlers, adults, the old: these children meet various ages and types most days and learn how to respond appropriately to them. It is striking that home educated children display better social skills than those of schoolchildren (Shyers, 1992). They can interact with older adults as equals and are not embarrassed to sit on the floor and play with a group of toddlers. There is none of the mumbling and shrugging of shoulders; home educated teenagers are generally self-possessed and articulate.

School – A common frame of reference

The idea of home educated children as socially inept misfits is clearly a myth. But there is one way in which individuals educated at home cannot help but be in a sense outsiders. At the beginning of Chapter 1 I said that school is the one thing everybody has in common. This is true of almost everybody whom one meets and it is often the only thing which two strangers in Britain do have in common. They might come from completely different social strata, be of different ethnic origin, gender or age, but all of them will have attended school. This common background is such an integral part of our lives that we seldom even think of it. School dinners, PE lessons, breaking up for the summer holidays, playtime; these are simply part of everybody's personal history. How many of us have met an adult in the UK who has never been to school? This shared experience of childhood shapes us in many ways, but the home educated child misses out on this, both the good and the bad. Some home educated young people have remarked that they feel a little left out when their contemporaries are talking about childhood.

It may not be a serious disadvantage for an adult in later life, but home educated children's childhoods are completely different from everybody else's. Lacking the common cultural heritage of school and all that is associated with it must have some effect upon the developing young person.

For example, most of us have to get up in the mornings and go to work. Having been accustomed to getting up at the same time each morning to go to school throughout childhood, we find the experience of getting up and going to work is not all that different. We have become used to doing boring and repetitive things that we would prefer to avoid. This is a benefit of regular attendance at school. The need to adapt to the wishes of others, to get used to a routine, to stick at a dull task – these are valuable habits for the developing child to acquire. Holt (1964) tells of a mother who, when he was working as a primary school teacher in New York, told him:

> I think you are making a mistake in trying to make the schoolwork so interesting for the children. After all, they are going to have to spend most of their lives doing things they don't like and they might as well get used to it now. (Holt, 1964)

Holt tells this anecdote in horror, as an example of clearly wrongheaded thinking, but this unnamed woman may have had a point.

Routines are comforting for children and it is no bad thing to become accustomed in childhood to undertaking activities which we would prefer to avoid. This, after all, is what much of real life is like. Perhaps it is poor preparation for adult life to allow children and teenagers to stay in bed as late as they wish; maybe it will become a habit?

Home educators argue that this idea of the benefits to youngsters of routines like getting up early and making their way to school as being good practice for the world of work which they must soon enter, does not stand up to scrutiny. It is true many home educated teenagers probably get up later than those attending school. There is evidence that, because as they grow the diurnal/nocturnal cycle is disrupted in youth, it is natural for young people to get up later than adults (Foster, 2007). The sleep pattern settles down as they become adults so there is no reason to suppose that home educated children will be unable to get up in time to go to work in later life. Meanwhile, they are simply being given the liberty to allow their bodies to make necessary adjustments at a crucial stage in their development.

Home educators question though to what extent school is good training for real life in the outside world. The idea that school is in some way a preparation for the outside world is not really borne out by the structure of school life. Where in the outside world, with the possible exceptions of armies and prisons, will an individual be dragooned into a squad of thirty others and expected to do precisely the same things at exactly the same time as everybody else, week in week out? Expected to seek permission for even so basic a human need as visiting the lavatory? A home educated child who had never spent a day in school enrolled at a Further Education College to study for A levels. She reported with astonishment that the single greatest feature of higher education for the students in her class was the freedom to void their bladders when they needed to, unlike when they were in school. This student was also amazed to hear her fellow students calling the lecturers 'Sir'. These two incidents alone suggest that school is hardly a good preparation for the real world.

Safeguarding
The danger of abuse

Home education invariably comes to public attention not because of educational problems but as a result of safeguarding concerns. The Khyra Ishaq case, culminating in 2010 with the trial of her mother and subsequent publication of the Serious Case review and the Badman review in 2009 both focused upon the harm which might befall children who were not attending school. Of the four terms of reference for Badman's review of elective home education, only one was actually concerned with education. The others related to either the *Every Child Matters* outcomes or the possibility of abuse. Home educating parents were particularly angered by the notion that their children might be at increased risk of abuse. Graham Badman found absolutely no evidence for this assertion and made this clear:

> I can find no evidence that elective home education is a particular factor in the removal of children to forced marriage, servitude or trafficking or for inappropriate abusive activities. (Badman, 2009)

Despite the bizarre phrasing of this statement, the conclusion is unambiguous: no evidence was found for any of the fears raised when the review was initiated. This did not prevent a subsequent attempt to claim that the numbers of home educated children known to children's social care were disproportionately high, although actual numbers were tiny in absolute terms.

Nevertheless, the fear persists that keeping a child at home makes abuse or neglect easier to carry out and harder for others to detect. The cases of Victoria Climbié, the Spry children and Khyra Ishaq are cited as examples of what can happen to children who are not at school. It is darkly hinted that lower levels of neglect and abuse might be more common. Allegations like this make some parents want to have nothing to do with anybody from the educational establishment.

Regarding these three cases, home educators make the following points. Victoria Climbié, who was mentioned by the NSPCC during the Badman review, was not and never had been home educated. Moreover, she and her guardian were well known to various services. In the weeks before her death Victoria had been seen by a doctor and both social workers and police officers had visited her home. None of the professionals who dealt with the child and her aunt guessed that she was about to be murdered. It is unlikely that an officer monitoring home education would have proved any more prescient. In other words, Victoria Climbié was not 'hidden', a word sometimes used when talking of home educating children. She had been seen and her home visited by a number of agencies. It did not prevent her death.

Eunice Spry was a home educator who was hideously cruel to the children in her care and later received a sentence of fourteen years imprisonment. What role, if any, did home education have in enabling this woman to torture and abuse the children for whom she had responsibility? These children too were not hidden – the local authority monitored their education by visiting the home twice a year and the children were regularly seen by healthcare professionals. Nonetheless, the abuse continued undetected for years.

Khyra Ishaq was withdrawn from her school, according to her mother, to be educated at home. There was uneasiness at her school when her mother declared her intention to home educate her seven year old daughter. Visits were made to the family home, although the child was only briefly seen on the doorstep by an officer from the local authority. A few months later, she had starved to death.

The case of Khyra Ishaq was cited as a trump card by during hearings at the CSF select committee in 2009. Paul Holmes MP, a member of the select committee, asked Maggie Atkinson, then Director of Children's Services in Gateshead and now Children's Commissioner, what her thoughts were on the possibility that rather than protecting children's interests, the legislation based upon the Badman report might instead be trampling over the interests of home educated children. Her reply is worth quoting in full, 'I would give you two words and they are the first and second names of the child who died – Khyra Ishaq' (CSF select committee, 2009).

The implication was that this one case alone justified all the recommendations made by Badman and the subsequent changes in the legal position for home educators. It is hard to know how to answer this. Children have in the past been starved, tortured and murdered by their parents and guardians and almost all of them have been registered pupils at schools. In many cases, children who are mistreated in this way are known to social services: they are not hidden from sight.

These arguments notwithstanding, it remains the case that being seen at school provides another layer of protection to children. It ensures regular overview by professionals who may well spot problems and be able to offer help or notify the relevant agencies. It is instructive in this context to consider the case of a five year-old child in Cheltenham in 2008. In a misguided attempt to discipline him and discourage him from biting his baby sister, his mother bit him on the arm, badly enough to leave ugly marks which were still visible a few days later. These were observed at school and action was taken. The mother was arrested and eventually received a sentence of five months imprisonment for assault (*Daily Mail*, 2008).

If this boy had been home educated, this abuse would almost certainly not have come to light. It would have been a simple matter for his mother to keep him indoors until the marks faded or make sure that he wore long sleeves to cover his arms. Children at school are seen regularly during PE, in the swimming pool and playground. Teachers can see if a child is covered in bruises, is dirty or smelly, if he wears inappropriately thin and inadequate clothes in cold weather, if he is unkempt, uncared for or starving. It is a rough and ready safety net which probably catches a fair number of neglected and abused children and prevents worse harm ultimately befalling them.

None of this is an argument against home education *per se*. It is rather cause for thinking about the adequacy or otherwise of the laws which currently cover home education and the removal of children, or failure to register them, at school. Another example from the recent past illustrates this point. In 1971, a little girl of eight was removed from school by her stepmother because, she said, the child's natural mother intended to take her back to their home in Scotland and enroll her at school there. The child was next seen twenty three years later when her decomposed corpse was dug from the floor of a house in Gloucester. Charmaine West was the daughter of serial killer, Fred West (*Independent*, 1995).

The ease with which Rosemary West had been able to take the child from school in order for her to be murdered provides a compelling illustration of the weakness of the current situation with children moving homes and schools: they can simply disappear and nobody is any the wiser. That children can just drop out of sight as Charmaine West did, is worrying. Any family moving district could still shed a child or two *en route* and as things stand now nobody would notice. ContactPoint would have addressed this problem but this was switched off in the summer of 2010. For this reason, regardless of the issues of educational benefit, the proposals of the CSF Bill for the registration of those taught out of school were welcomed by many professionals.

In 2010 Ofsted published a survey undertaken in fifteen English local authorities. They discovered that thousands of children went missing every year, local authorities simply had no idea where they went or what happened to them. One rural authority was aware in the spring of 2009 of over a thousand children who had vanished from schools and might be missing from education. By the autumn, half of these children had still not been found. Doubtless, most had simply moved to other local authority areas, but others could be receiving no education at all or even no longer be alive: the local authorities had no idea (Ofsted, 2010).

None of the above safeguarding issues are arguments for or against home education as such. They constitute elements in the debate upon the extent to which society has a right to monitor children, its most vulnerable members, and ensure that they are safe and well. There is probably a stronger case still to make for the closer scrutiny of home education in the case of children known to other agencies such as social services.

Professional fears
In Chapter 2 we looked at some of the fears that local authorities had regarding home educated children who might be hidden from view. There was anxiety about possible abuse and the feeling that it was im-

possible to know if such children were receiving an efficient education. Another concern was touched upon, that local authorities are afraid that home educated children will sue the authority when they become adults, for not ensuring that they were being provided by their parents with a suitable and efficient education. There is also the fear that a home educated child will be abused or murdered and that some civil servant or local government officer will be blamed. These apprehensions are seldom voiced publicly and so it was refreshing to hear Peter Traves of the Association of Directors of Children's Services speak honestly about this when giving evidence at the CSF select committee in October 2009. He said:

> If something happens to a child in terms of any of those five outcomes, we are held directly to account. This is not some kind of button counting. We have seen recently what happens to directors of children's services when things go seriously wrong. It is not only a case of sacking; it is public humiliation. It is a very serious matter. (CSF select committee report, 2009)

This was presumably a reference to the treatment of Sharon Shoesmith, former Director of Children's Services for the London Borough of Haringey. Ms Shoesmith was sacked following the case of Baby P, a little boy who was killed in appalling circumstances. The murder of a toddler is also a 'very serious matter', although not apparently as serious as the public humiliation of a Director of Children's Services. In short, some professionals fear that they will lose their jobs if a home educated child comes to harm.

Other safeguarding concerns

One of the major reasons for parents de-registering their children from school is the perceived inability of schools to meet their child's special educational needs. When Ofsted conducted their survey of home education in late 2009, the inspectors spoke to the parents of 130 children. A quarter of these either had a statement of special needs or when de-registered had been at the stage known as 'school action plus', meaning that they needed extra support to cope with a special educational need (Ofsted, 2010). Other surveys have similarly found a high proportion of home educated children with special needs (Hopwood *et al*, 2007).

Children with statements and identified for 'school action plus' need extra help and support. Yet as we have seen, all support typically ends when they are removed from school (CSF select committee, 2009). Whether this is the parents' fault for de-registering them, or the school's for not making arrangements for the support of occupational therapists and so on to continue once the children have been removed from the school roll, the fact is that these are vulnerable children in need of services which they no longer receive.

There is another, more general, concern about children who are not attending school. Teachers are trained to spot developmental problems and learning difficulties. They are professionals who are likely to know if a child is having more trouble acquiring some skill than others of a similar age. In this way mild difficulties like dyslexia and ADHD might be noticed and appropriate action taken. More serious learning difficulties are also identified and referrals made to specialist services. The child who is not regularly seen by a teacher misses out on this. She may well fail to learn effectively because of something as trifling as a slight hearing impairment or even a more serious problem such as brain damage. Home educated children do not have to be seen by any professionals; some do not have hearing or sight tests. Even short-sightedness can be a barrier to education if not identified and treated while the child is young. All these things are far more likely to come to light in children at school than they are in children whose parents might not arrange for the necessary routine screening.

The parents' perspective

The current confusion among professionals between purely educational concerns and children's safety and wellbeing has created more ill feeling than any other aspect of the home education debate and it is vital that this issue is resolved. When Graham Badman started his review, his terms of reference spoke specifically of home education being used as a cover for child abuse (see Chapter 5). There was also much mention of the five desirable outcomes of the *Every Child Matters* document, despite the irrelevance to home educated children of the third outcome: 'Enjoying and achieving so that children are ready for school, attend and enjoy school'. Bringing these outcomes into the question of home education makes it unclear whether home education is being seen as an educational or a child safety issue.

Home educating parents point out that there is no reason to suppose that children are at risk when home with their parents any more than school children are when they go home after school ends. Surely we assume that children are in general safe with their parents during the weekend or school holidays. Nobody wishes to inspect the homes and investigate the family circumstances of three year-old children at home with their parents. Why should the situation be thought to change suddenly when they reach their fifth birthday? Are children in general thought to be safe when at home with their parents and, if not, should the families of schoolchildren be regularly checked and their homes inspected during school holidays? Until this issue is tackled to the satisfaction of both parents and local authorities, relations between home educating parents and those who are monitoring them will be strained.

Qualifications
Home educators and GCSEs
In contrast to children at school, almost all of whom take at least some GCSEs, it is not at all uncommon for home educated children not to take a single GCSE. No central records are kept, but when individual local authorities release data, these are not encouraging. In 2009 Dudley, a town in central England, revealed that of the hundred home educated children known to the local authority only half had taken any GCSEs. Nationally, over 98 per cent of pupils sit at least one GCSE. Fewer than one in ten of the home educated children attained at least five GCSEs at grades A*-C, including mathematics and English, a fifth of the national figure (*Express and Star*, 2009).

There are several reasons for this poor performance – a performance which is probably typical of most local authorities. The major reason is that proportionally fewer home educated children sit GCSEs in the first place. This is due to:

- the financial cost of taking the examinations
- difficulty in finding an examination centre
- ideological objections to studying for examinations
- a belief that GCSEs are unimportant
- inability of some parents to teach effectively to GCSE level

- difficulties with coursework
- a belief that GCSEs can be taken at colleges later

Until 2010 the cost to a parent of their child sitting a single GCSE or IGCSE ranged from £80 to £150. With rare exceptions, the examinations were taken at independent schools, which charged the market rate for their services. This could mean a parent paying upwards of £1000 for her child to take eight or ten GCSEs. This figure is beyond the means of many parents so their children reached the age of sixteen without taking any GCSEs. Fortunately, the Charity Commission's attempts to ensure that independent schools with charitable status provide 'public benefits' has had the effect of forcing down the cost of sitting examinations. An increasing number of independent schools now welcome private candidates and charge them £40 or £50 to sit a GCSE.

However, not all schools and colleges welcome private candidates. Some have had difficult experiences with home educating parents. Most parents are not as familiar as teachers and other professionals with the process for taking GCSEs. Another problem is that many home educated children have special educational needs which must be catered for during examinations. They might require scribes, separate rooms, keyboards or extra time. All these complicate matters for schools and have led to some being reluctant to take private candidates. The result is that parents sometimes have to travel for miles so that their children can sit examinations and possibly stay overnight in another city. All this adds considerably to the cost.

Autonomously educating parents would only arrange for their children to take examinations if they were specifically asked to do so. Since this is a major strand in British home education, it means that a high proportion of such children will not take any examinations.

Moreover, not all parents are capable of teaching effectively at the level needed for GCSE. It requires a thorough familiarity with the course specification and the ability for both parent and child to put in many long hours of work. It is a daunting prospect for many parents and of those who do undertake GCESs, many restrict them to one or two: typically mathematics and English.

It has proved hard in the past for parents to authenticate coursework for GCSE. The move to controlled assessments in the classroom will make this all but impossible. This is one of the reasons why IGCSEs are generally preferred to the GCSE.

There is a belief among home educators that their children might be able to take GCSEs at Further Education colleges when they are sixteen. Unfortunately, most FE colleges now limit GCSEs either to re-sits for those who did badly at school or to courses aimed at overseas students.

One matter has been the subject of much misunderstanding and has serious consequences for young people's life chances. The myth that it is possible to enter university without taking GCSEs or A levels is long-standing and widespread among home educators. We know that many children who have attended school go on to attend colleges and universities. We know that many go on to become solicitors, doctors, architects and accountants. There is little evidence that it is true of adults who were home educated and took no examinations. With all the debate over home education, such individuals would have surely come forward to proclaim that they became lawyers or surgeons without setting foot in school. This is suggestive evidence but not conclusive. But the rarity of professional attainment is bourne out by the way that the same one or two cases of academic success are quoted whenever home educating parents seek to defend their lifestyle.

One young man gained a place at Oxford University to study Law despite never having taken any GCSEs or A levels. This was managed partly because he had been studying with the Open University, but he had also been working for several years in a solicitors' office to gain experience. How did a teenager without any GCSEs get to work in a solicitors' office like that? The answer is that his father is a lawyer. This case is often cited with various details omitted to make it look as though getting into Oxford without GCSEs or A levels happens all the time. There was also a home educated boy in Manchester who gained a university place to study bio-medicine. Neither of these young men were educated entirely at home. The one who went to Oxford attended school until the age of eight and the one who studied bio-medicine studied for formal qualifications at college when he was fourteen.

Anybody asking about the post-sixteen prospects for home educated children will be sure to hear about these cases – but only these. If it were more common for home educated young people to gain access to university without formal qualifications, we would surely have heard more about it. It is true that universities place on their websites the alluring prospect that they will consider favourably applications from those without conventional qualifications such as GCSEs or A levels. In practice this is often aimed at mature students or those from overseas, who have other formal qualifications such as the International Baccalaureate. Such declarations make the universities appear to be widening their admissions criteria – but few young people gain admission to a university without some qualifications.

Home educated children who do sit GCSEs or IGCSEs have many advantages over their schooled peers. The main one is that they do not have to sit ten or twelve examinations over the space of a few weeks. There are two sessions each year for sitting International GCSEs, allowing one or two to be taken in May and a couple more in November. They can be spread over a few years. Home educated children who do sit examinations in this way can easily take the first one or two when they are fourteen, so that no more than three at the most are taken in any one session.

Home educating parents point out that not all children at maintained schools achieve splendid results in their GCSEs. They argue that if the government is worried about the education of children, they might be better advised to improve the standards of the schools which 99 per cent of children in Britain attend. Rather than being so exercised over the educational attainment of a few tens of thousands of home educated children, they should concern themselves with the millions of school-children who, as official figures show, are failing to fulfil their potential.

Alternative qualifications
GCSEs or IGCSEs are the standard qualification in Britain for people under the age of seventeen, but there are others. Some teenagers sit National Tests in Adult Literacy and Numeracy. Level 2 of these tests is supposedly the equivalent of a good GCSE. Others opt for Open University courses. In the summer of 2010, an eighteen year old girl who had never been to school was offered a place at Exeter University on the

strength of 190 points gained through studying with the OU. Taking Open University courses seems to be becoming increasingly popular with home educated children and could provide them with an effective route into higher education.

Home educated young people who are Not in Education Employment or Training

The failure to take GCSEs can have dramatic and long lasting effects upon a child's future. An increasing number of Further Education Colleges now require a student wishing to study A levels to already have passed five GCSEs. There is anecdotal evidence that colleges and sixth forms are no longer prepared to be flexible about a lack of GCSEs. Some courses in subjects like performing arts and photography might be accessed via auditions or portfolios, but the child without any GCSEs would find himself barred from the study of more traditional or academic subjects.

Potential employers too look askance at the job applicant who lacks a single GCSE. According to one survey, 20 per cent of employers would not even consider a job applicant with no GCSEs at all (LSC survey, 2006). How can they be sure that this person possesses even the rudimentary literacy skills that a Grade C English GCSE more or less guarantees? Opting not to enter for any examinations can cast a long shadow.

During the meeting of the CSF Commons select committee in October 2009, it was said that there were a disproportionate number of NEETs among home educated youths – those Not in Education, Employment or Training. This caused a good deal of anger among home educators, for the following reason. We make certain assumptions about children who have attended school to the age of sixteen by looking at what they are found to be doing when they are age sixteen to eighteen. So if a seventeen year-old has a job, then all is well; he is in employment. If she is studying for A levels at the local sixth form or Further Education College, then she is in education.

As a consequence, because the number of NEETs includes all young people who are not actually registered with a sixth form or college nor in training or employment, all teenagers who have been educated at home up until the age of sixteen and are still studying independently of any school or college are placed in this category. As home educating parents are not slow to point out, this is absurd. If their child has been learning at home and continues to do so after sixteen, why should she suddenly be counted among the dropouts and failures? One boy who sat and passed eleven International GCSEs with outstanding grades and then decided to study for A levels at home had, his mother discovered, been officially recorded as a NEET.

However, it is rare for home educated children to study for A levels at home and it does seem likely that proportionally fewer home educated teenagers are employed or at college than among those who attended school.

Religion and ethnicity
Concerns about 'indoctrination'

Some parents in Britain do home educate for religious reasons, but it is almost certainly less prevalent than in America. Religion is not commonly cited in surveys about home education in the UK. However, the very possibility that religion could be a motive for home education alarms some people. In a written submission to the Badman enquiry, the British Humanist Association raised concerns that 'Some of those who choose to educate their children at home for religious reasons may not be providing schooling which is adequate' (Badman Report, 2009).

It feared that that parents might be indoctrinating their children into one narrow religious perspective and thereby cutting them off from society. Jehovah's Witnesses, for example, might teach their children that the rest of the world is wicked and that they should avoid making friends with those of other faiths or with atheists.

The Church of England, too, expressed concerns in its submission to Badman.

> Children who do not go to school may not experience the social and cultural diversity encountered there; they will not learn to deal with the rough and tumble of everyday life; they may never meet people with different faith and value systems. (Badman Report, 2009)

The Church of England went on to endorse the government's Community Cohesion Programme and expressed concern about the possibility that children taught at home might not be encouraged to question their own beliefs and practices. A number of parents who chose to educate their children at home for religious reasons found this an extraordinary point of view for a Christian church to adopt.

This issue has become a matter of increasing concern in the US because religion, more specifically Christianity, is a major factor in the decision to home educate. In 2009, a court in New Hampshire ordered a ten year-old home educated girl to be sent to school on grounds that the girl, 'appeared to reflect her mother's rigidity on questions of faith' and that the girl's interests, 'would be best served by exposure to a public school' (New Hampshire Public Radio, 2009).

Home educators in Britain are watching closely to see whether this sort of ruling will become common in America. Judging by some of the submissions made during the Badman enquiry, there are certainly people who would welcome this. Similar cases have been seen in Europe. In Sweden the child of a home educating Christian couple was taken into care in 2009, and several Christian families in Germany have been prosecuted for refusing to send their children to school.

Nobody has remarked that bringing up a child inevitably indoctrinates him with his parents' views and opinions on religion. The nominally Christian parents who do not take their child to church on Sunday or say grace before each meal are making a statement about their values. Not having a Bible in the bookshelf says as much about a household as does having one on display. There is no such thing as a neutral religious upbringing. All parents, whether or not they are home educators, whether they practice a religion or are atheists, give their children messages about what their attitude towards religion is expected to be. What most people regard as a neutral religious background really means no religion at all, which is quite a different thing.

School can be good for children in respect of religion. Children are exposed to a wide range of ideas which they may not encounter at home, from the theory of evolution all the way through to the fact that society believes that homosexual behaviour is acceptable. In some homes, those of fundamentalist Christians and Muslims for example, the children might not be exposed to either of these ideas.

But children may well meet with other ideas that they would not find at home. They may learn from their schoolmates that strong people can bully and torment weaker ones, or that it is OK to steal from shops. Equally they may find that some people enjoy poetry, that playing a team game is fun and that most people are pretty much the same regardless of their cultural heritage. It is possible that they might not have discovered these things had they stayed only in the company of their parents and siblings.

Gypsy/Roma home educators

A substantial proportion of home educated children in Britain are of Gypsy/Roma heritage. In a research paper for the Department of Education and Science, it was stated that:

> Few Gypsy/Roma and Traveller parents have the knowledge, skills and resources to provide or deliver a full-time education that is efficient and suitable. (Ivatts, 2006)

The author went on to say:

> The legal context now requires a legislative amendment to the previous weak arrangements. The DfES needs to address the issues and take action to safeguard the interests and welfare of the very vulnerable children in these communities, and indeed, all those children being educated under the EHE arrangements. (Ivatts, 2006)

Many children from the Gypsy/Roma/Traveller community are being educated outside the school system and this has caused concern. Traditionally, this group values practical skills over academic achievement. Current monitoring of educational provision relies upon the goodwill of all involved. This is difficult enough with families living in a fixed location: with those following a semi-nomadic lifestyle, it is more difficult. Ofsted observed recently: 'Gypsy/Roma and Travellers of Irish heritage have by far the highest rate of absence from school and the highest exclusion rates of any ethnic group' (Ofsted, 2010).

A particular issue is the education of the girls. There is a suspicion that girls of this community are provided with no formal education after the age of eleven (CSF select Committee, 2009). Since they lack any real statutory powers, local authority officers sometimes rely upon bluff to persuade parents to cooperate with monitoring. Such tactics are unlikely to succeed with members of this community and there is little that local authorities can do to check on educational provision.

Muslim home educators

Anecdotal evidence suggests that an increasing number of Muslims are educating their children at home. This appears to be for the same general reasons which motivate some devout Christians that is to say, a desire to protect their children from what they see as a corrupt and secular society. Some religious parents view peer pressure as not just an irritating fact of life but a baleful influence which tends to draw young people away from their families, culture and beliefs.

We noted that one of the terms of reference for the Badman review concerned forced marriages. This relates to a problem associated exclusively with girls whose families originate from the Indian sub-continent. The fear is that a girl de-registered from school for the ostensible purpose of home education is liable to be whisked off to Pakistan or Bangladesh for an arranged marriage. Despite the fact that Badman found no evidence at all for this (Badman, 2009), the fear still exists among some local authorities remains, particularly those with large communities of South Asian origin.

There is also a wider fear about the development of separate communities within our larger cities. In the calls for community cohesion, suggestions are made that Muslim children being taught at home or in exclusively Muslim schools would create a deep divide with the wider society.

7

Ways forward for home education

Local authorities, as we have seen frequently have very different perspectives on home education. So different are these positions that disputes and continuing hostility between them might seem inevitable. This chapter sketches out a possible way forward and suggests a model of home education which might be satisfactory to everyone involved, in whatever capacity.

Any model of home education with a realistic chance of being accepted would have to take into account the concerns of professionals in the field of education and welfare, but also cater for the sensitivities of the parents and children themselves. I believe there is such middle ground. In order to reach it, both parents and professionals must expect to make compromises.

There are certain teaching unions who do not think that home education should even be an option and who would like to see all children taught in school. Among the submissions received by Badman was one from the National Association of Schoolmasters/Union of Women Teachers, which said:

> The NASUWT maintains the existence of a right to home educate is anomalous with the clear emphasis in Government policy of ensuring that all children and young people can benefit from educational provision where teaching and learning is led by qualified teachers in well resourced and fit for purpose modern educational settings. (Badman report, 2009)

The Association of Teachers and Lecturers stated, 'The ATL believes schools are the best place for a rounded education – including social education' (Johnson, 2009).

These are hardly disinterested commentators. For most of us, the state run education system in the UK is as tight a monopoly as can be imagined. Unless you are fortunate enough to have a good deal of money to spare, it is the local maintained school for your child. Now that ordinary parents are becoming more widely aware of a viable alternative they are beginning to vote with their feet. Like all monopoly holders, teachers view this situation with alarm. If we assume that there are eighty thousand children being educated at home, that means the loss of, or failure to build, over a hundred schools. That is quite a few teaching posts lost.

In America the National Education Association, the union which represents teachers and professional educators, has raised a number of objections to home education (NEA, 2007). Among them are some which we have already looked at: concern about socialisation with those of other races or faiths, the potential for the development of religious extremism and the possibility of poor academic achievement. They are also concerned about 'reduced funding for public schools'. Home educators view this anxiety as meaning that teachers are worried about the loss of jobs.

It might also be irritating for British teachers to see people teaching without being burdened by all the familiar paraphernalia of CRB checks, risk assessments, the National Curriculum, targets, policies, guidelines, tests, reports and inspections. They see home educators as free to concentrate wholly upon teaching.

At the other end of the debate are the more militant and vociferous parents, who see any attempt to monitor their provision as next door to totalitarianism. Somewhere between these two positions lie the great mass of parents and professionals, almost all of whom would be happy to reach an accommodation which was acceptable to everybody.

Many in the world of conventional education would like to see home education subjected to similar controls to those which apply to schools. They would like to see home educated children tested and their parents' ability to provide a suitable education for their children examined and critically evaluated. Those found wanting would be compelled to return their children to the school system. Most of those who feel this way have no wish to end home education or prevent it from being a possible option for parents, but they believe the present system to be slack and inefficient and liable to fail children.

Many parents, on the other hand, want to be left to their own devices and a large number are opposed to anybody judging them or their children. Most of these parents might grudgingly accept visits from local authority officers, but only if they get something in return. They need a motive to become engaged with their local authority, other than being refused registration if they do not toe the line. However, some parents do not want anybody in their home under any circumstances or conditions, particularly those who have withdrawn their children from school because they feel that the school has failed their children by not tackling bullying or having failed to make adequate provision for their special educational needs.

Before outlining the features needed for a successful system of monitoring and supporting home education, it is useful to look at the experience of the Australian state of Tasmania. The arrangements there might possibly be adapted for Britain and provide a suitable basis for a monitoring regime which would satisfy both parents and professionals. But there is likely to be resistance.

When Badman was reviewing home education, he discussed how the monitoring of home education had been undertaken in Tasmania since 1993. This was received with so little enthusiasm that in his report Badman conceded that it might have been 'a step too far'.

While the review took place, many home educators were hoping that the status quo would prevail. They seemed to think that if they told Badman that home education was working effectively and that no changes were needed, his report would end up as a series of vague recommendations which would not be binding. There were good grounds for this optimism. Following York Consulting's study in 2006, guidelines on home education were produced for local authorities which did nothing to alter the legal situation and were generally ignored. So Badman's ideas were dismissed out of hand as being unworkable, unsuitable, irrelevant or unacceptable to the great mass of home educating parents.

It was a bold bluff but clearly things are not going to stay the same. The CSF Bill may have been passed without the clauses on home education, because of the general election, but Ofsted repeated the demand for compulsory registration only weeks after the new government took office. A month later, the Serious Case Review into the death of Khyra Ishaq was published and this too recommended new restrictions on home education (Radford, 2010). Parents may do better to work together with the Department for Education and local authorities in constructing a model for monitoring which would be workable and broadly acceptable to all. If they do not, then a system for the regulation of home education may be imposed upon them.

The Tasmanian Model

Tasmania, a large island off the coast of Australia, is a state of Australia with a population of around half a million, half of whom live in the capital city of Hobart. In 1993, the Minister of Education in Tasmania set up the Tasmanian Home Education Advisory Council (THEAC). This body oversees home education on the island, including registration and monitoring. It has no connection with the Ministry of Education, but is directly answerable to the Minister of Education in person. The council has six members, three of whom are home educators and three who have been appointed by the Minister of Education from the wider community. They pay a small staff to register and monitor home education.

The figures involved are telling. At the last count, Tasmania had almost seven hundred home educators, about the same number as in some English counties. The THEAC employ only two staff to monitor educational provision, a similar number to those engaged many English counties, despite the disparity in the area covered. In all, the figures for Tasmania and its elective home education service in general approximate to the statistics for many English counties.

The great advantage of the Tasmanian system is that it is run primarily by home educators themselves. One of the chief complaints which parents in the UK level against those who monitor their educational provision is that that those carrying out the monitoring do not understand how home education works – a fair point. Many, perhaps most, of the local authority officers who currently monitor home education come from a teaching background and so are inevitably used to judging education against a school model and might be unsympathetic to teaching which does not closely approximate to this model.

In Tasmania, the entire monitoring system, together with the criteria for what represents a successful education, has been devised by home educators. It is a system designed and implemented by home educators, for home educators.

There were two reasons why nobody expressed any interest in the Tasmanian Model during the Badman review. One was that it was devoutly hoped by many that the situation in Britain would not change. The other relates to the politics of the home education world.

When the idea of the Tasmanian Model was tentatively suggested by Badman, it was inevitable that the support group Education Otherwise should be suggested as the ideal partner in any such enterprise. Education Otherwise has been going for over thirty years and many connected with home education see it as the authentic voice of home educators. In recent years, however, other groups have started in Britain, and there have been internal problems in Education Otherwise. So any new model which featured Education Otherwise in a prominent role would automatically alienate a large number of other home educators. The mention of Education Otherwise as a possible major player gave the Tasmanian Model the kiss of death.

The need for research

To design a new model of home education monitoring which will be broadly acceptable to most parents and professionals, we need to find out more about why parents are drawn to the idea of educating their children out of school. Previous research has, as we saw, given us strong clues but we need to know more conclusively just what motivates parents to choose this path. In particular, we must discover what is driving the huge growth in home education over the last few years. Access to information and support on the Internet certainly provided a boost in the late 1990s but this is not enough to explain why the figures are still climbing steadily.

The first step in approaching the situation would therefore be a survey of all home educators in several local authority areas. Previous surveys have relied upon self-selection and tiny samples. Some have been limited to families of whom the local authority is aware, others were restricted to members of home education support groups: all have been completely voluntary. York Consulting for example, selected nine local authority areas for their study, a third of which had disproportionately large numbers of Gypsy/Roma/Traveller families (Hopwood *et al*, 2007). This led to accusations that their research was flawed. What must be done is for every single home educating parent and child in several varied and disparate districts to be sensitively questioned about the reason for their choice. These data must be cross checked with school and social services records to build up a complete profile of the home educating community.

This in itself might initially cause difficulty as many home educating parents are suspicious about questions and surveys. They always suspect that there is an ulterior motive to the obvious one of wishing to improve services for children. We have seen that when questionnaires are distributed to home educators, a 20 per cent response rate is counted as good. This attitude makes it hard to work out what is really going on in the world of home education and what home educators actually want.

Towards the end of 2009 Ofsted began conducting a pilot survey of home educating parents known to their local authority in fifteen local authority areas (see Chapter 4). There was a great deal of suspicion about this project, with a number of parents determined to have no part in it. Offence was taken at questions aimed at finding out what sort of hobbies and outside activities children engaged in, there was anger at a question which asked whether or not children worked for set hours each day, and bitterness at Ofsted's assumption that children would routinely be sitting GCSEs. Their attempt to find out what home educating parents were doing was seen as an unwarrantable intrusion. On more than one Internet list for home educators, appeals were made for parents not to co-operate with this survey and it was strongly hinted that those who did so were betraying other home educators.

In February 2010, the DCSF announced the setting up of a longitudinal study which would investigate the possibility of tracking educational attainments and outcomes for home educated children. This proposal too was greeted with suspicion by many home educating parents.

Because of such difficulties, gathering the information necessary to plan and implement a national system for the supervision of home education may need to be done without seeking the permission of those involved. Most professionals who have looked seriously at home education in recent years agree that compulsory registration is essential (Ivatts, 2006; Badman, 2009; Ofsted, 2010; Redford, 2010). It is also generally accepted that only half of all home educating families are known to local authorities (Hopwood *et al*, 2007; Badman, 2009). Compulsory registration would allow us to find out the whereabouts and enquire into the motivations of every home educating parent in Britain. With such information, an accurate picture of home education as it is practiced in the UK could be built and appropriate services could be planned.

Pedagogy
The strengths of home education

Home education, however it is carried out, is completely different from school. Most of the techniques used to teach groups of thirty children at a time are irrelevant to the practice of home education. There are good reasons why a 'one size fits all' philosophy has had to develop in schools. The education in British schools is designed for the mass instruction of young people and when working with large groups of children, collaborative learning is often the most practical pedagogical approach. This means that all the children are learning the same thing at the same time. However, when teaching one or two children in a domestic setting, personalised learning backed up by unlimited one-to-one tuition becomes possible. Teaching is conducted by somebody with an intimate knowledge of the child's strengths and weaknesses and who is familiar with her learning style. Questions can be answered immediately and any misunderstandings dealt with at once. Every lesson is individually tailored to the needs of that particular child.

It is easy when educating at home to switch seamlessly from one approach to another. This can happen in the course of a few hours. In the morning, problem-based learning might take place while working on a scientific investigation. After lunch, perhaps learning will be more free ranging as the child works on some scheme of his own choosing. Not only do different children have different learning styles, their preferred method of learning can change from subject to subject. In school, changing moods and preferences cannot be so readily taken into account, whereas at home it is easy.

As mentioned in Chapter 1, many wealthy families preferred this type of one-to-one education for their children in the nineteenth and twentieth centuries. A governess living and working on the premises delivered personalised education to a small number of children. This approach can be equally efficient when conducted by a parent.

The freedom to vary and adapt the education being provided in light of circumstance is highly prized by home educators. In a school, each lesson must be planned weeks in advance and there is little chance for spontaneity. At home, plans can be changed or abandoned at a moment's notice and a different teaching style adopted to fit any change in the situation. To give a specific example, my daughter was studying hard one day in January 2006, focusing upon biology. When news came that a whale had become stranded in the Thames though, we were able to drop everything and race into London to observe this rare event, which tied in perfectly with our studies of mammalian biology. She moved in a couple of hours from reading about sea mammals to observing a whale plume in real life. Such impromptu field trips are not an option for a class of thirty children.

Structured and unstructured education

As we have seen, some home educators are strictly structured while others are very relaxed and prefer not to plan lessons in advance. There is also a good deal of overlap between the two styles. Although some home educators are teachers, most are lay people with little interest in pedagogy and their decision not to send their children to school is often part of a lifestyle choice rather than purely an educational matter. The only educational philosophy explicitly embraced by British home educators is that known as autonomous education.

Autonomous education

This form of education is a form of Inquiry-based Learning. It is child-led and in many cases even the decision about whether or not to learn to read is left to the child rather than directed by the parent. Such educators eschew all plans and curricula, insisting that their children alone must decide what they wish to learn and when they will learn it. Rigid adherence to this approach has caused much friction between the parents who champion it and the local authorities charged with monitoring the education provided. Any system of monitoring and supervision, however lax and easy going, will bring local authorities into conflict with such parents. A future scheme for regulating home education will have to take this into account and, if necessary, will need to be implemented without too much regard for the sensitivities of the more extreme members of this group.

Aims
The rights of the child

Any monitoring regime for home education should have one aim: securing for children their statutory right to a suitable and efficient full-time education. Both Graham Badman and the last two Secretaries of State for Education referred at times to the 'right' of parents to home educate – but there is and can be no such right. This idea, that the rights of the child must be balanced against the 'rights' of the parent, has arisen through faulty logic. The 1996 Education Act lays a duty upon parents to cause their children to receive an education. Because the parents have a duty, this has the effect of creating a right for the child, the right to an education, but no corresponding 'right' is created for the parent.

A suitable and efficient education

The education children must receive is one which is efficient, full-time and suitable to their age, ability and aptitude and also to any special educational needs they may have. There is no definition of what is meant by these terms. We are obliged to examine old court cases to discover what might be meant by a 'suitable' education. Edwardian court transcripts a century old are not the ideal guide to what is meant by a 'suitable and efficient education'. Before the 2010 general election the DCSF was actively considering formulating a definition of what constitutes a 'suitable education'. Once we have the definition, it will give local authority officers a yardstick against which to measure the education being provided for home educated children.

Abolishing home education 'by default'

Badman spoke in his report of home education 'by default' (see Chapter 2). He was referring to parents who have not made a positive decision to home educate but felt manoeuvred into it by circumstances. We know that a large proportion of children being educated at home have been withdrawn from school for reasons such as bullying, school refusal and the perceived inadequacy of the provision made for special educational needs (Rothermel, 2002; Hopwood *et al*, 2007). These are not ideologically motivated home educators who have since their children's birth been determined to undertake their education single handed. These are ordinary parents who were content to send their children to school like everybody else. But at some stage their child's school failed to meet their expectations and after matters reached crisis point they reacted by pulling the child out of conventional education. It is safe to assume that if the school had met the parents' and children's expectations, these children would not have been de-registered.

Interestingly, many parents who have withdrawn their children for such reasons say that even if the problems which prompted this extreme move were now rectified they would still continue to home educate.

As discussed, certain schools and local authorities are known to have collaborated with parents in order to rid themselves of persistent truants or troublesome pupils, by encouraging them to de-register their children on the pretext that they would be home educated. It is possible that similar arrangements might be made over children whose parents are constantly complaining to the school. The school is likely to welcome the parent's decision to give up on school and home educate instead.

There is currently no stigma for a school if parents choose to de-register their children in order to home educate. Some schools do not even report this to the local authority. High truancy figures and exclusions, however, reflect badly on schools, and to avoid this, some schools are found to encourage parents to home educate (Davies, 2000; CSF select committee, 2009; Ofsted, 2010). A change of perspective is needed, so that children being removed in order to be educated at home are regarded in the same way as truancy and exclusions: as something out of the ordinary which needs to be investigated.

This could in part be achieved by implementing the recommendation made by Badman calling for the Children's Trust Board to be sent annual returns listing the numbers of home educated children in the local authority's area. Schools should be expected to inform their local authority when pupils are de-registered for the purpose of home education. If schools were given strong incentives to tackle the problems which cause increasing numbers of parents to withdraw their children from mainstream education, the number of parents home educating might fall. Once children are taken out of school, they seldom go back. So every effort should be made to prevent situations reaching the point where parents feel that they have no choice but to take their child out of school.

Fifteen or twenty years ago many parents in such situations would not have contemplated home education. That school attendance was not a legal requirement was not widely known. But home education should not be a soft option just because all it takes is to send the local authority an educational philosophy, decline a visit and then do as much or as little as they wish about their child's education. The option of home education should not be chosen because it is the path of least resistance. Home education is not and should never be any less demanding and rigorous than school based education.

By requiring greater accountability from both schools and parents, the current rise in elective home education could be halted and even reversed. The aim should be for schools and local authorities to feel that it is their fault if parents become so dissatisfied with the school's provision that they feel compelled to withdraw a pupil. At the same time, parents have to realise that de-registering their child is not an easy way out since teaching her at home will be time consuming and demanding. Monitoring and registration should be ways of showing parents that de-registration is a very serious step and that their child will not be left to his own devices if withdrawn from school.

Disaffected youths who do not wish to remain in school and who regularly truant or disrupt classes are sometimes de-registered, ostensibly in order to be educated at home. There is some evidence that certain schools and local authorities collude in deceptions of this sort and actively encourage parents to withdraw their children from school for the school's benefit rather than for the child. Ofsted (2010) cites their own report, *Children missing from education*. During a survey of local authorities they found one in which two schools had instructed parents to de-register their children ostensibly in order to educate them at home.

It is generally accepted that for some teenagers school is not the best place, but that does not mean that the best place for them is slouching around the house and receiving no education. Home education should always be a positive choice and never a default way of solving difficulties at school, be they truancy, bullying or any other issue.

Curriculum
Planning the education

Some home educators are resistant to anything resembling a curriculum. Badman's suggestion that parents should provide a statement outlining what they hoped to achieve with their children's education in the forthcoming year was met with dismay and refusal to accept the idea. But this position does not hold up either legally or logically. All parents hope that their children will learn to read, write and be able to perform basic arithmetical operations. Most probably hope that the children will manage this before the age of eleven. Just establishing this common ground means that parents are, by implication, acknowledging the need for a curriculum, however rudimentary.

Some home educators agree with John Holt's view that 'since we can't know what knowledge will be needed in the future, it is senseless to try and teach it in advance' (Holt, 1964). However, educational professionals agree that a statement of **educational approach** must be central to a parent's decision to educate a child at home. It should indicate which subjects will be covered and give some idea of the techniques which will be used to teach them. Badman envisaged no more than two sides of A4 paper, setting out only what the parent hoped the child would cover in the next year – perhaps 'to begin reading independently in the coming year'.

The legal position is clear: parents have a duty to provide their children with an 'efficient' education. In a landmark ruling, Mr Justice Woolf declared that an 'efficient' education is one that 'achieves what it sets out to achieve' (Woolf, 1985). Unless one knows what one is setting out to achieve, it will be impossible to know if one has achieved it. Another case which has bearing upon the matter is *Harrison and Harrison v Stevenson*:

> In our judgement 'education' demands at least an element of supervision; merely to allow a child to follow its own devices in the hope that it will acquire knowledge by imitation, experiment or experience in its own way and in its own good time is neither systematic nor instructive. Such a course would not be education but, at best, child-minding. (*Harrison and Harrison v Stevenson*, 1981)

These key cases clearly support the need for a plan for the education of a child taught out of school. Both imply that planning and preparation will be needed and also clarification about what it is hoped to achieve.

Assessment

Home educating parents often argue that it should be assumed that they are furnishing their children with a satisfactory education unless there is strong evidence to the contrary. However, the 1996 Education Act lays upon parents a duty to cause their children to receive an education. Since this duty is a sense thrust upon them, it is reasonable that checks are made to ensure that they are fulfilling this duty.

A statement by parents of their educational approach for the coming year is of little use if nobody will be checking to see how far their hopes for the year are fulfilled. An inspection should cover not only the extent to which parents were able to accomplish their stated educational aims over the last year, but should also evaluate how well the child is achieving in comparison with pupils of the same age at school. If a child of thirteen is, say, unable to read, he needs help, whether or not his parents have expressed anxiety.

Assessment is currently undertaken by local authority officers, many of whom are ex-teachers. Some are sympathetic to home education; others strongly disapprove. Different local authorities have different standards and there is no agreed measure by which to determine whether or not a parent is providing a suitable education. Ofsted has been suggested for this role, but many parents do not think that an organisation which inspects schools could be expected to understand home education. A new inspectorate is needed, specifically to inspect home education, as suggested below.

Examinations

That proportionally fewer home educated children than children at school take GCESs is unsatisfactory. Firstly, lack of GCSEs diminishes the chances of gaining employment and makes it more likely that young people will become NEETs. Secondly, it makes it harder for them to move into higher education, restricting them to non-academic and vocational courses. This runs counter to the definition of a suitable education, laid down by Mr Justice Woolf as one which:

> ... primarily equips a child for life within the community of which he is a member, rather than the way of life in the country as a whole, as long as it does not foreclose the child's options in later years to adopt some other form of life if he wishes to do so. (Woolf, 1985)

Failing to study for and then sit examinations such as GCSEs does indeed 'foreclose the child's options in later years'. The aim should be for all home educated children to have the same opportunities as other children, including the chance to enter higher education if they wish, but failure to take GCSEs curtails their life chances.

Accountability
Duties of parents

The duty of parents is to cause their children to receive an efficient education suitable for their age and their special educational needs, if any (Education Act, 1996). Accordingly, parents should be held to account if they fail to do so. Action needs to be swiftly taken against parents who fail to give their children an education or refuse to provide evidence that a suitable education is taking place.

The role of local authorities

Local authorities in the UK have wide ranging responsibilities towards the children in their area, not least seeing that they receive an education and ensuring that they are safe and well. Currently, local authorities are unable to fulfil some of these duties because they do not know the whereabouts or even the number of children living in their area, as demonstrated in the Ofsted report on children missing from education (Ofsted, 2010). New legislation is needed so that the whereabouts and educational setting of every child in England can be established and children can no longer drop out of education without anybody knowing. It must give local authorities the powers to check that every child receiving an education.

Support

A sizeable number of home educated children have **special educational needs** of some kind. Because almost all children are at school, that is where virtually all provision is made for services such as Speech and Language Therapy and Occupational Therapy. Educational Psychologists and other professionals work closely with the schools. When a child is de-registered from school, these services may stop abruptly. The Ofsted survey (see Chapter 4) shows that many parents who take children who have special educational needs out of school, are aggrieved at being deprived of these services.

It is already possible for parents to make their own referrals for Speech Therapy and special dentists, via hospitals and health centres, but few know how to do so. So when a child with special needs is withdrawn from school, the services she is receiving often cease.

Once home education becomes overseen by the local authority and thus a part of mainstream education, these services could be accessed by families as easily as if their children were still at school. Music, sports, Speech Therapy, Occupational Therapy, laboratory facilities and all other services need to be fully accessible to home educators.

Access to **work experience** is generally not available to home educated children because of the insurance. Employers prefer to deal directly with the local authority on this matter. Places at Further Education Colleges for vocational courses should similarly be made accessible to families more directly.

A good many home educating parents would welcome practical help and **advice from experts** such as teachers and psychologists. Teaching one's child can be lonely and sometimes unnerving. Most parents, even the most confident, need reassurance and support from time to time.

Some belong to organisations like Education Otherwise and meet other parents in person. Others rely upon online communities for support and this can present a difficulty. The big online groups in the UK, those with thousands of members, are slanted towards an autonomous perspective. Since home educating parents are looking for objective help and advice, an online community is needed which is run by both home educators and educational professionals. Parents with questions about anything from the legal position surrounding home education to the age at which a child should be reading independently could then hear the views of both teachers and home educators. At present, several of the most popular support groups on the Internet bar professionals from membership. So myths, half truths and outright falsehoods can flourish.

Support is also needed towards the cost of **examinations**. When assessing the long term impact that the new regulations on home education contained in the aborted CSF Bill, the DCSF spoke of the advantages to everybody if home educated children began passing five GCSEs at grades A* to C (DCSF, 2009). If parents must continue to pay for each GCSE, while the schooled child pays nothing, it is unlikely that masses of home educated children will sit, let alone pass five GCSEs. Suggestions about how examinations and the other resources discussed in this section would be paid for are offered below.

A possible model for home education in the UK

A system of home education and monitoring would only prove acceptable to home educators in Britain if, as in the Tasmanian model, they themselves are centrally involved in setting it up and running it. Monitoring will always be open to the charge that those doing it do not understand home education and do not appreciate the differences between home education and schooling unless it is done by teams which include home educating parents.

Home educators need to be involved in a central council which is responsible for home education across the whole of the United Kingdom. But basing it in London might not be acceptable, particularly for those in remote parts of the country. A family teaching their child in the Hebrides might feel that people in London did not understand the issues involved in home education in the Western Isles of Scotland. So location will be an issue.

Although there are broad trends in home education, purposes and practices vary as greatly as the parents undertaking it and these too vary geographically. A parent in the Western Isles, for instance, might want to teach her daughter for a year or two before sending her to secondary school at the age of eleven. This is likely to be different from what parents in metropolitan boroughs in London or Manchester will be planning for the home education of their children.

So the best approach might be to set up local Home Education Advisory Councils, composed partly of home educating parents who understand the concerns of parents in their own area. This would also make it difficult for a single national organisation to dominate the initiative, as was feared by some parents when the idea of a council was first mooted by Graham Badman. A small council could devote its energies entirely to its proper business: the registration and monitoring of home educators within a delineated geographical area.

All that would be needed to form a council of this sort would be a legal requirement to notify the local authority of an intention to home educate. Once all home educators are identified, some independent body could circulate nomination forms and ballot papers to all the parents of home educated children in the local authority area, so that three or four parents could be chosen by local home educating parents.

As in Tasmania, local home education advisory councils would be made up partly of home educators and partly of people from the local community. Together they would agree protocols for monitoring home educators living in the area, working within the framework of any new legislation, but allowing a good deal of latitude for individual arrangements. A setup like this would draw the poison from the festering relationships between some home educators and their local authority. They would be dealing not with some local government apparatchik but with parents who educated their own children and knew the specific problems faced by home educating parents in the district.

Relations between home educators are more cordial in some areas than others. In Hampshire, for instance, home educating parents have meetings with councillors and officers of the local authority to try and reach agreement on various policies which affect home education. Informal arrangements of this kind can offer a model for a council of the kind envisaged.

Other local authorities also provide examples of good practice. North Yorkshire County Council runs regular sessions where home educating parents and children can meet, attended also by education professionals who can give help and advice if needed. They will also help parents and children plan routes into college and university.

Somerset County Council too works closely with home educated children. They pay for and help to arrange examinations for children who have been registered with their local authority for more than two years. They also work with Further Education Colleges to help find placements for home educated children on both vocational and academic courses. And they put on workshops for home educators on literacy and numeracy.

These examples illustrate that with a little effort and a deal of good will, formal councils made up of home educators, education professionals and local authority officers could be established. As long as these councils were run jointly by professionals and parents and had real powers, this would improve the relationship between home educating parents and their local authority.

Home education advisory councils of this sort, based upon the Tasmanian model, along with new legislation which at last puts home education on a recognised legal footing, would establish home education as a legitimate choice for parents. It would put paid to the view that elective home education should be squeezed or legislated out of existence and that all children should be taught in school. Far from damaging home education, as some parents fear, the recommendations of the Badman report would establish home education firmly as a serious choice in modern education. Had Schedule 1 of the Children, Schools and Families Bill 2009 become law, home education would have been explicitly recognised as a legal choice and parents would no longer have to rely upon hundred year old court cases and vague sentences in various Education Acts to exercise this option for their children.

Paying for a system
Elective home education is presently run on a shoestring because central government in Westminster does not provide local authorities with the Age Weighted Pupil Unit or AWPU which they give for every

pupil registered at a maintained school. This amount varies currently from £2152 a year for children in Year 1 to £3530 for those in year 11. Parents who teach their own children are still paying income tax and council tax and if their children were at school, the local authority would be receiving the AWPU each year to subsidise their children's education. Instead, all expense must currently be borne by the parent – from pencils and exercise books to examination fees. Yet each child educated entirely at home saves the state over £27,000.

Quite apart from the goodwill that providing this money would surely create among home educators, it is a matter of natural justice, as well as common sense. New legislation aimed to raise the standard of educational provision made for home educated children would have to be properly funded. Central government needs to provide the appropriate AWPU to local authorities for every home educated child of whom they are aware. Home educated children must be able to access the same services and sit the same examinations as school-going children, without paying to do so.

Conclusion

This book has shown that home education, delivered with rigour, can be an effective preparation for adult life. Properly conducted, this kind of education can provide an education as good as that furnished by the best schools. It has been argued here that the benefits to children of being raised at home rather than being sent to be taught by strangers can be immense. Every child has the right to an education. And parents, who have no rights in the matter, have the duty and the responsibility to ensure that their children receive the effective education which is theirs by right.

References

Alverstone, Lord; Richard Webster (1911) *Judgement in Bevis v Shears*

Badman, Graham (2009) *Review of Elective Home Education in England*. London: The Stationery Office,

Baker, Joy (1964) *Children in Chancery*. London: Hutchinson

Bell, David (2004) Lecture at Hermitage School. BBC report 5/10/04

BBC News Report (2002) Former pupils lose bullying claim 5/7/02

BBC News Report (2005) Growth market in home education 18/3/05

BBC News Report (2009) Home educators are angry at review 19/1/09

Bowlby, John (1979) *The Making and Breaking of Affectional Bonds*. London: Tavistock Publications

Brussels Journal (2006) European Human Rights Court Upholds Nazi Ban on Home-schooling 28/9/06

Children, Schools and Families Bill (2009) *House of Commons Bills 8 2009-10*. London: The Stationery Office

Children Schools and Families Committee (2009) *The Review of Elective Home Education*. London: The Stationery Office

Chitty, Antonia (2008) *What to do when your Child hates School*. London: White Ladder

Colorado Department of Education (1963) *Revised Statutes: Education Article 33, School Attendance Law of 1963*

Cunningham, Hugh (2006) *The Invention of Childhood*. London: BBC Books

Daily Mail (2008) Mother Jailed for Biting her Five Year Old Son 23/9/08

Davies, Nick (2000) *The School Report*. London: Vintage

Department for Children, Schools and Families and the Ministry of Justice (2009) *Impact Assessment the Children Schools and Families Bill 2009*. London: DCSF

Des Moine Register (2004) Home schooled do well at Iowa's universities 14/12/04

Durbin, Deborah (2009) *Home Education*. London: Hodder Education

Education Act 1996 (1996) London: Crown copyright, Her Majesty's Stationery Office

Education (Pupil Registration) (England) Regulations 2006, Statutory Instrument 2006 No. 1751 London: TSO

Express and Star (2009) Home-schooled pupils fall off radar 19/12/09

Farris Michael P (1997) Solid Evidence to support Home Schooling. *Wall Street Journal* 5/3/97

Forster, W E (1870) *Speech in* Parliament. London: Hansard

Fortune-Wood, M (2005) *The Face of Home-Based Education.* Nottingham: Educational Heretics Press

Foster, Russell: Interviewed in *Evening Standard* (*Evening Standard,* London 12/1/07)

Furedi, Frank: Interviewed for BBC News (BBC News online 19/11/09)

Gidney, Dave (2003) *Children in the Heart of God.* London: Kingsway Communications

Goodman, Paul (1962) *Compulsory Miseducation.* New York: Horizon Press

Guardian (2000) News report 13/8/2000)

Harrison, Iris (1981) Diary (Given in evidence at Worcester Crown Court)

Harrison and Harrison v Stevenson (1981) QB (DC) 729/81

Head, David (Editor) (1974) *Free Way to Learning.* London: Penguin Education

Hirsch, E.D. (2006) *The Knowledge Deficit.* New York: Houghton Mifflin

Holt, John (1964) *How Children Fail.* New York: Pitman Publishing

Holt, John (1981) *Teach Your Own.* New York: Delacourt

Hopwood,V, O'Neill, L, Castro, G, Hodgson, B (2007) *The Prevalence of Home Education in England: A Feasibility Study Research Report 827, 2007* (2007) London: Department for Education and Science

Independent (1995) News Report on West case 22/11/95

Independent (2009) We must get tough on Home Schooling 30/7/09

Ivatts, A (2006) *Elective Home Education: the situation regarding current policy, provision and practice in Elective Home Education for Gypsy, Roma and Traveller Children.* London: DfES Research report RW77

Johnson, Martin (2009) Interview by Children and Young People. *Now Magazine.* 28/1/09

Learning and Skills Council (2006) *Survey of Employers.* London

Mill, John Stuart (1873) *Autobiography,* London

Moore, Dorothy and Raymond (1975) *Better Late than Early.* New York: Readers Digest Association

Moore, Dorothy and Raymond (1981) *Home Grown Kids.* New York: Word Books

Mountney, Ross (2009) *Learning Without School.* London: Jessica Kingsley

National Education Association (2007) *Annual Meeting of National Education Association*

Neil, A S (1960) *Summerhill.* New York: Hart

Neufeld, Gordon and Gabe Mate (2004) *Hold on to your Kids.* New York: Ballantine

REFERENCES

Newcastle Report (1861) *The State of Popular Education in Britain*. London

New Hampshire Public Radio News Report 9/9/09

New York Times (2010) Judge grants asylum to home schoolers. New York, 28/2/10

Ofsted (2010) *Local authorities and home education. Ref. No. 090267*. London: Ofsted

Ofsted (2010) *Children missing from education. Ref. 100041*. London: Ofsted

Taylor, L A and Petrie, A J (2000) Home Education Regulations in Europe and Recent UK Research. *Peabody Journal of Education* 75 (12)

Phillips v Brown (1980) Divisional Court June 20th, Lord Donaldson

Popper, Karl (1976) *Unended Quest*. London: Fontana

Radford, John (2010) *Serious Case Review in respect of the death of a child, Case number 14*. Birmingham: Birmingham Safeguarding Children Board

Ray, Brian D (1997) *Strengths of their own: home schoolers across America*. Oregon: National Home Education Research Institute Publications

Ray, Brian D (2003) *Home-schooling Grows Up*. Oregon: National Home Education Research Institute

Rothermel, Paula (1998) *Times Educational Supplement* 25/9/98. London

Rothermel, Paula (1998) *Home Educating: a critical evaluation*. Exeter: British Psychological Society Annual Education Conference

Rothermel, Paula (2000) The Third Way in Education: Thinking the Unthinkable. *Education 3-13*, Volume 28, No. 1, March Staffordshire: Trentham

Rothermel, Paula (2002) Home Education; Rationales, Practices and Outcomes. PhD dissertation Durham: University of Durham

Rudner, L (1999) Achievement and Demographics of Home School Students. *Education Policy Analysis Archives* Volume 7, No 8

Rutter, Michael and Smith, David J (1995) *Psychosocial Disorders in Young people: Time Trends and Their Causes*. New York: John Wiley and Sons

Shyers, Larry (1992) Comparison of Social Adjustment between Home and Traditionally School Students. Florida: University of Florida, Ph.D Dissertation

Taunton Report (1868) *The Schools Inquiry Commission*. London

Thomas, Alan (1994) Conversational learning. *Oxford Review of Education* 10, 131-142

Thomas, Alan and Lowe, Jane (2002) *Educating Your Child at Home*. London: Continuum

Thomas, Alan and Pattison, Harriet (2008) *How Children Learn at Home*. London: Continuum

Times Educational Supplement (1999) Working Class Children Top Home Study League 30/6/99

Times Educational Supplement (2009) Should Home Educators face greater scrutiny? 31/7/09

United Nations (1989) *United Nations Convention on the Rights of the Child*, UNCRC. New York

United States Department of Education (2008) *National Household Education Survey 2007, National Centre for Education Statistics.* Washington

United States Department of Education (1999) *Homeschooling in the United States 1999.* Washington

Walmsley, Jane and Margolis, Jonathon (1987) *Hot House People.* London: Pan Books

Webb, Julie (1990) *Children Learning at Home.* Basingstoke: Falmer

Woolf, Mr Justice (1985) *Judgement in R v Secretary of State for Education, ex Parte Talmud Torah Machzikei Hadass School Trust*

Index